Praise for
The Gain Principle

"Steve Pruett's *The Gain Principle* is more than a career-transformation book. It's a life-transformation book. Having had the honor of knowing Steve for over sixteen years, I have long been in awe of his professional wisdom and personal fortitude. Throughout this book, Steve combines unvarnished personal stories with insightful self-reflection exercises to create an inspiring road map for supercharging your own journey to success. It's a fantastic read!"

CARRIE RADOVICH, executive and leadership coach

"*The Gain Principle* will be a game-changer for any aspiring business leader or executive. From the first page, you feel like you're sitting down with an old friend who is sharing the playbook to his incredible journey. Steve's insights on how to navigate from a modest start to the top echelons of the media world are both profound and practical. His "GAIN" system—Go, Assess, Identify, and Next—is a testament to his thoughtful analysis of success, born from decades of real-world experience. What I love about this book is its authenticity. Steve doesn't just recount his wins; he dives into the challenges and lessons learned along the way. Whether you're a young professional at a crossroads or a seasoned executive looking for fresh inspiration, this book offers an approach that is as motivating as it is actionable. Steve's storytelling is compelling, with rich anecdotes that make you feel the highs and lows of his journey. His reflections on pivotal moments and the people who influenced him are particularly resonant. This isn't just a business book; it's a guide to personal and professional growth that's grounded in the real-life trials and triumphs of a media titan. Highly recommended for anyone serious about leveling up their career and life. I can't wait to read it again!"

JOE MECHLINSKI, *New York Times* bestselling author and CEO of SHIFT

"*The Gain Principle* can immediately transform the way you lead and live. I've had the pleasure of working directly with Steve and have seen his framework in action. If you work it, it will work for you. The growth cycles of Go, Assess, Identify, and Next are simple, straightforward, and transferable. The most game-changing element that Steve shares is leapfrogging. Readers and leaders will learn how to bring massive transformation to their lives and to their organizations. Simple. Clear. Effective. *The Gain Principle* is a must-read and must-apply for anyone seeking to achieve sustained success."

ANDREW FREEDMAN, bestselling author and managing partner

"In *The Gain Principle*, Steve Pruett takes us on the remarkable journey of his career and shows us how we can be equally successful in any area we choose. From his good but humble origins in the backwoods of Arkansas to the rarified boardrooms of New York, whether in the c-suite of Sinclair Broadcasting or as the executive chairman of Cox Media Group. Mr. Pruett has seen it all: the early days of UHF television, the glory days of cable and retrans, to today's world of streaming. But *The Gain Principle* is more than a memoir—much more—because Mr. Pruett has been more than an executive. He's also been a leader, mentor, and coach, and *The Gain Principle* is also a road map for success. He distills the ideas and actions that helped make him so successful into one word: GAIN, which stands for Go, Assess, Identify, Next. Following his framework can be as life-changing for you as it has been for him. If you only read one book this year, read *The Gain Principle*."

CHARLIE McLRAVY, CEO, fiction writer

"Steve Pruett's personal mentorship transformed my career. In this candid book, Pruett shares the framework that propelled his remarkable rise in the media industry: the growth cycles of Go, Assess, Identify, and Next. Applying these principles to my own career unlocked opportunities and growth that I never imagined possible. *The Gain Principle* is an indispensable guide for anyone striving to optimize their potential and achieve enduring success."

FRANKIE RUSSO, bestselling author and eight-time *Inc.* 500 Entrepreneur

"Over the past few months, I've been experiencing a lot of change. I decided to evaluate and guide myself based on the GAIN model that Steve's wonderful book *The Gain Principle* outlines so clearly. As entrepreneurs, sometimes we rest on our laurels and past successes. This lulls us into a comfort zone that can cause complacency, lost customers, and revenue and process breakdowns. Using the GAIN model, I knew I had to make a decision and Go. I Assessed my options with perspectives from past key clients, internal leaders, and team members of my company, an executive coach who has known me for thirty-plus years. Then I Identified a new approach for key messaging, new processes, and a plan to move forward in each of these areas by getting my team involved and on board. And now I am living Next by refining and carrying out our new messaging. I can now add one more step in my Next stage: what strategic partner can best help me execute and carry out this plan. Steve's book has been with me every step of the way. It couldn't have come at a better time in my business life cycle. I recommend this to everyone in a leadership position who desires to do more and be their best throughout their career."

MICHAEL W. KUBLIN, president, PeopleTek Inc., and Amazon bestselling author of *The Leadership Lessons of Howard Stern*

www.amplifypublishinggroup.com

The Gain Principle:
Mastering Life's Growth Cycles for Success and Service

©2025 Steven J. Pruett. All Rights Reserved. No part of this publication may be reproduced, stored in a retrieval system or transmitted in any form by any means electronic, mechanical, or photocopying, recording or otherwise without the permission of the author.

All photos courtesy of the author.

For more information, please contact:
Amplify Publishing, an imprint of Amplify Publishing Group
620 Herndon Parkway, Suite 220
Herndon, VA 20170
info@amplifypublishing.com

Library of Congress Control Number: 2024907037

CPSIA Code: PRV0824A

ISBN-13: 978-1-63755-479-1

Printed in the United States

To Paula, for the gift she has been to me for over forty years, and to our two sons who have passed away but made a substantial impact on many people during their too-short time. We had an active, vibrant relationship with them for twenty and thirty-five years, respectively. Family is an integral part of the Gain Principle process and has always been my primary motivator.

Alex

Stefan

Steven J. Pruett
Executive Chairman, Cox Media Group

The Gain Principle

Mastering Life's Growth Cycles for Success and Service

Contents

Introduction: How Did I Get Here?   1
Prologue: From the Outhouse to the Penthouse   5
A Guide to GAIN   19

PART ONE
INTRODUCING GROWTH CYCLES

    Chapter 1: The GAIN Model for Growth   31
    Chapter 2: Looking for Leapfrog Moments   59
    Chapter 3: Learning from Failure   81
    Chapter 4: The Importance of Resilience and Persistence   97

PART TWO
APPLYING GROWTH CYCLES

    Chapter 5: Growth Cycles in Action   113
    Chapter 6: Overcoming Barriers to Growth   135
    Chapter 7: Influencers   149
    Chapter 8: Making Growth Cycles Your Own   167

Acknowledgments   185
Music Credits   187
About the Author   189

Introduction

How Did I Get Here?

> And you may find yourself living in a shotgun shack
> And you may find yourself in another part of the world
> And you may find yourself behind the wheel of a large automobile
> And you may find yourself in a beautiful house, with a beautiful wife
> And you may ask yourself, "Well, how did I get here?"
> —**Talking Heads, "Once in a Lifetime"**

This book is not meant to be the story of my time as a top-level c-suite executive at Sinclair or executive chairman of Cox Media Group, but the two scenes that follow do set the stage for my message. How can a person like me go from a modest, working-class upbringing to the highest levels of responsibility and position in the industry I chose as career? The answers are too many to count, but I can share a system that worked for me. I would like to say I figured this system out early on, but truly I only came to understand it after I began to analyze my career as I've gotten older. I've identified a set of actions that I've repeated over and over again without fail in virtually every meaningful situation I've encountered over a nearly fifty-year career in media and telecommunications.

What I discovered when I analyzed my journey is that these four steps were a constant throughout all of my cycles of growth: Go, Assess, Identify, and Next.

Win or lose, I've stayed with the system I now call GAIN.

Scene 1

It's April 2019. I am sitting in a junior suite at the Wynn Hotel in Las Vegas with Brian Brady, who is one of my best friends, and two young men who are partners at Apollo Global Management, which at the time was the largest private equity buyout fund in the world. Brian had created a new broadcast venture that led Apollo to swoop in and invest in buying his company and spending an additional $4 billion to acquire some of the most premium TV and radio stations in the United States.

The focus of this discussion would become a big opportunity at a point in my career when I thought I had already achieved the bulk of my goals. I would later figure out that getting an hour of time with David Sambur and Aaron Sobel was something tens if not hundreds of network and broadcast executives wanted but most could not get.

Eventually through working with them, I learned that their attention spans were incredibly short and they were impressed by almost no one. Both were in their thirties and impressively smart, informed, and experienced, with the ability and inclination to quickly judge what they were being served as either meaningful or BS. By August 2019, I was in Atlanta preparing for the takeover of Cox Media Group, which Apollo had acquired from the privately held behemoth, Cox Enterprises, a true gem of a company. Cox was managed by some of the most down-to-earth and genuinely kind people I have ever met. My job was to get the existing management to adapt to the standards of performance required by a PE-owned company in order to meet the required return on investment typical of buyout funds. My title was executive chairman.

Scene 2

Eight years earlier, I had a similar meeting with David Smith, the self-made billionaire who built Sinclair Broadcasting from a family-owned company to a publicly held broadcast giant with more than two hundred stations. At the time of the meeting, Sinclair had about forty-five markets and ninety stations. I was pitching David on investing in my venture to acquire a small station group where I was the CEO. His first question to me was, "What do I need you for? I can just do this without you."

Clearly I had a good answer, because he agreed to invest in forming a new company, Chesapeake Television, with me to acquire TV stations in smaller markets. We went on to acquire sixty stations in forty markets for a little under a billion dollars and then merge them into Sinclair in 2014 with me becoming co-COO of all of Sinclair. By believing in me and making a rather unorthodox decision, David created what until then was my greatest opportunity in business and leveraged my career to unexpected heights, which ultimately put me into the room with Apollo in Las Vegas in 2019.

What do these stories have in common? The principles I outline in GAIN that you are about to learn.

Prologue

From the Outhouse to the Penthouse

> I never was alone
> Long enough to know
> If I ever was a child.
> —**Wilco, "If I Ever Was a Child"**

While this is not a memoir and I don't intend to revisit my entire life, you must look at your childhood in order to understand your foundation to grow, so we will take a look at mine. Most of the things that form your approach to life happened to you as a child. It is worth assessing.

As I made my way from my modest, working-class, farm-raised beginnings to the rarefied surroundings of high-level finance, corporate boardrooms, and c-suite-level presentations, one way I would reality-check myself is to think to myself, "I bet no one in this room ever regularly used an outhouse growing up because they had no other option." It was my way of level-setting and seeing what many would consider adversity as an advantage.

I assume that, if you've picked up this book, you are motivated and willing to work hard to achieve your goals. Motivation, hard work, and the desire to achieve are table stakes. As my good friend Ann Ellis, a successful leader, says, "You can't teach 'want to.'" By no means do you need to decide early in life what you want your future to be, but it is helpful to have a grasp on how far you want to go and what you are willing to sacrifice to get there.

People often ask a perplexing question about my business journey. In one form or another, they ask, "How did you get to where you are today?" I am the chairman of a multibillion-dollar US media company, that's true—but I'm definitely not the richest, the most famous, or the most brilliant person in this (or any other) business. Despite coming from a blue-collar, working-class upbringing, I did manage to build a very successful career that took me to the c-suite of a Fortune 500 media company and eventually to the executive chairman role of a major media company owned by one of the largest buyout funds in the world.

Some who ask are people I work with every day. Many are young, ambitious up-and-comers. Perhaps they imagine themselves as future media executives. Some are old friends and people I've gotten to know along the way. Others are just new to the chaos of the media business today. Maybe they're just looking for some friendly advice. I'm happy to help, of course, but sometimes it can be hard to put my answer into words.

When people ask me that question, I often think what they really want to ask is, "How can *I* do something like you did?" They don't want to *be* me, but they want to achieve their own success. As you'll see in the book, these kinds of questions are the beginning of a new cycle of growth.

As you can imagine, the media business is constantly under intense public, private, and regulatory scrutiny. But somehow I managed to maintain a prominent profile and a record of success. I've been able to generate a lot of income and amass a modest amount of wealth. If you smooth it all over it looks very nice, but believe me, there are plenty of ups and downs.

Lately, the question has made me think: How *did* I get here? More importantly, how can I tell my story and explain my process in a way that makes sense to you—that will help you understand and apply the same principles I used to get to the penthouse. When I started out, I didn't have a specific goal in mind except that I wanted to "make things happen."

Along the way, I have been an owner of TV and radio stations, a media investment banker, a founder of a successful digital media company, a large-company c-suite executive, and, finally, executive chairman of a large PE-owned company. I have been on boards of all types and had experiences and met people I could not have dreamed of down on the farm. Now I have a real desire to help others achieve more than they even think is possible. What always surfaces from people who have worked with me is how much I want to help others learn and succeed. This book is the first step of formalizing that desire into action. It's my own Next, which is also a Go moment (but we'll get to that in a bit).

With some trepidation, I decided to write about my journey, as a guide for those facing their own challenges. I decided to write a book describing the process I've learned over the years—an action plan, if you will—to help motivated people like you learn how to generate your own success, your own upward mobility, no matter what stands in your way.

The main purpose of this book is to help those who are at an inflection point in their careers. Perhaps they are facing change or a new opportunity. Perhaps they are like you. Hopefully, the tools presented in this book will help facilitate that process of change with greater confidence and effectiveness.

The best way to explain the "how" of my journey, to myself and by extension to those asking the question, is to start with my personal story. I wasn't born to great wealth or social standing. I presently live in what is by today's standards a modest penthouse in Atlanta, along with my permanent home in Arizona. But I was born worlds away, in Lawrence, Kansas. I grew up in rural Arkansas and then in Dupo, Illinois, just south of East St. Louis. My parents were factory shift workers—union employees for General Motors. My childhood did not prepare me for a life in business. While my parents wanted me to go to college, there was not a plan for how to do that. I ended up getting an athletic scholarship, the prospect of which began to surface in high school.

Shortly after I was born, since my parents had to live wherever there was work, everyone agreed that the best thing was for me to stay with Grandmother in Arkansas. She had lived and worked there her whole life, running a small farm. Granddad, literally a woodsman from Arkansas, operated a sawmill nearby. Under the circumstances, life on a working farm under Grandmother's care was the very best thing for me . . . in more ways than one.

When I say Grandmother, I'm not being formal. That's just what I called her—no Gramma or Nana for me, just Grandmother. She was a truly amazing woman, and the first *master leader* I ever knew.

The daughter of settlers, she had grown up in the early twentieth century, building a family farm and growing it beyond mere subsistence. No doubt she had to deal with wolves, bears, and bandits who attacked their livestock and threatened their existence. By the time she married and started her own homestead, she was experienced and confident she could take care of it—and anything that came along with it.

Looking back at my three-year-old self, I realize how fortunate I truly was. Early on, I learned the value of *competence* fused with *confidence*. My dad was a mechanical genius who knew he could fix any machine. My mother was fiery and fearless in protecting the family. But as far as I was concerned, Grandmother Ruth ruled the world. Today, it's impossible to overestimate how much her simple life practices affected my own success and my career trajectory.

From the age of three, according to my earliest memories, I was allowed to roam free around the farm—under Grandmother's watchful eye. I "helped" with various chores and, by age four, was allowed to go by myself to fish in the nearby pond. Throughout my time there, she guided me through a number of childhood rites of passage, a few of which proved in hindsight to be highly instructional.

Eventually, the chores became more real, and I was given greater autonomy than many children of my generation—certainly more than children are afforded today. Even after I went back to live with my parents, my summers were spent on the farm. At the end of every school year, they put me on a train to Arkansas, by myself, to continue living and working with Grandmother. At age six, I was given a .22 rifle and allowed to roam the hundred-acre woods, hunting for squirrels and rabbits. Both on the farm and when I returned home for the school year, I was given a great deal of freedom to roam for hours on my bike, exploring the area and engaging, more or less innocently, with nature and society.

I realize all this sounds impossibly idyllic, but there were plenty of times when it was less so. My earliest memory, at age three, was in fact traumatic—at least to a three-year-old.

My father had been working at Granddad's sawmill. He was even considering becoming a business partner. But the reality was that a job at the auto factory in St. Louis was a far better opportunity, offering a chance at what he deemed a far better life. Once that was decided, Grandmother drove me from the farm to drop me off at our little green house by the sawmill so we could prepare for the move to the big city.

As soon as it dawned on me what was happening, I broke free from my mother's restraint and began running down the gravel road in hot pursuit of Grandmother's 1954 Studebaker. In my imagination, chasing her down that river rock road seemed like I was climbing through boulders, heedless of the danger. My three-year-old brain had not processed the risk, only the potential reward. I simply went for what I wanted, which was Grandmother. The results were what you might expect, a lot of grown-ups running, shouting, and waving their arms. Fortunately for me, she decided to stop and visit with a neighbor just a short distance down the road. But in my mind, I had "caught" her. Motivation had overpowered all thought.

What happened next was my first conscious exposure to a master of leadership. Once calm had been restored, Grandmother took me for a drive in her car. We rode around, talking, stopping at the store for a treat, and talking some more. Eventually she led me to accept a modified situation of going with my parents when the time came. She negotiated for me to stay with her until school started, which was two and a half years. It was time for a change, and change was good—even when you're only three. I went on to spend every summer with my grandmother until I was fifteen.

It was also my first inkling of a pattern, cultivated by Grandmother, that would serve me well over the years. That pattern includes a sense of *motivation* and negotiation in pursuing something I truly wanted, even when I didn't understand all the facts.

Grandmother was a magician when it came to getting me to act—or at least comply with the realities of farm life. Sometimes she resorted to outright trickery, convincing me to do things I really didn't want to do but somehow ended up doing anyway. She never discouraged my wayward motivation but time and again led me to pursue a course whose "payoff" was clear only after the fact.

Today, I'll admit that I occasionally act like a three-year-old, going for something I just *want* without considering the risks or weighing all the facts. In fact, there are those who work with me who also act like three-year-olds at times. But the real magic trick is to retain your motivation, that desire and willingness to put yourself on the line, potentially angering everyone you know, when everything inside you says "Go!" Sometimes doing so has a payoff, but the payoff is seldom what you expected.

Grandmother was also a master leader when it came to *overcoming fear*—probably the single greatest obstacle to your success in life. Before I was fully aware of my own growth cycles, and even at times when I was more self-aware, fear has been a deterrent, making each cycle longer and more difficult than it needed to be. But with each new lesson—with Grandmother and afterward—I have learned the true value of confidently facing those fears.

There were many things to be legitimately afraid of on Grandmother's farm, to say nothing of my Granddad's sawmill. There were bulls in the field, fractious chickens from whom I had to collect eggs, all sorts of territorial bees and wasps in the barn, not to mention water moccasins in the pond and copperheads in the woodpile. The sawmill was a whirling collection of engines, pulleys, flywheels, sawdust chains, and of course blades that could convert you quickly into compost.

But the greatest fear of all loomed in the backyard. Grandmother's farmhouse was without indoor plumbing. So, as you've probably guessed, my greatest fear was in the form of a monstrous and most unpleasant outhouse. This was my seminal lesson in overcoming fear in order to move ahead in life.

After the notorious Grandmother-catching incident, she and my parents struck a grand bargain, whereby I would stay with her in Arkansas until they were settled in St. Louis and it was time for me to go to school. One of Grandmother's duties before and during that period was to conclude that glorious rite of childhood passage—potty training. She undertook the duty with her usual skill and diplomacy. I suspect she was also driven by a strong sense of urgency, no doubt due to the lack of a modern washing machine and ample running water. I was quickly promoted from diapers to a chamber pot, which she took pains to make as pleasant an experience as possible for me. Her kind words of encouragement were genuine, but they were also training and rehearsal for the big solo event.

To a three-year-old, an outhouse is a truly scary thing. Frankly, it would be scary to almost anyone these days. Built from big slabs of barnwood, it had significant gaps between each slab, which made winter use quite the adventure. (In summer, the effect was considered a benefit.) Inside was a high bench with two dinner plate–sized, roughly sawn holes leading to the pit below. To a three-year-old, looking down into those holes was like gazing into the depths of hell. All sorts of horrible things could be down there, one imagined, including water moccasins or, God forbid, copperheads. (In hindsight, an outhouse pit is certainly the last place a self-respecting snake would consider home.) In fact, the outhouse *was* home to a teeming population of spiders—including black widows and brown recluses—as well as myriad other hazards, including a collection of splintered wood surfaces in inconvenient locations.

In the rural south, there were many stories—hopefully apocryphal—of kids being killed by water moccasins, copperheads, and other denizens of dark places. But the fact remains that, no matter what the true stories were, I was, if you'll excuse the language, scared shitless. However, since that was not literally the case, I had to overcome my fear. I had to take stock of my situation, and then learn and apply some new habits.

Grandmother had prepared me for the main event, but I had to act for myself. My initial attempts were less than ideal. She had prepared me to approach the building—assuring me that snakes would be dormant so late in the year and that it was similar to using the chamber pot. But my fears got the better of me. I "broke training" and decided to squat over the hole, forestalling any serpent's attempt to stage a rearguard action. But as I reached for the Sears catalog, my foot slipped part way into the hole. Screaming ensued as I tried to free my foot from the Devil's Den. Grandmother came to my rescue, but she did not just pull me out of the hole. Instead, she calmly told me how to get myself out and clean myself up.

This was the first time I began to realize how terror can focus your mind, but that your first reaction can be very wrong. When someone teaches you something, they probably know you won't listen carefully and will very likely do the wrong thing. In my case it was, literally, to "put my foot in it." Ideally, they help by talking you through your obstacle rather than doing your job for you. Most importantly, they also know that you're capable of learning, assessing the situation, and ultimately progressing to the next step in your journey.

There is one last Grandmother story that further illustrates aspects of a growth cycle, although I didn't know it at the time. Throughout the book, we'll see that we're usually unaware of the cyclical nature of our journey, and of the major moments and milestones along the way. That was certainly true for me.

From ages three through five, under my parents' and Grandmother's grand bargain (actually just common sense), I stayed mainly at her Arkansas farm until it was time for me to start school. I moved to St. Louis with my parents, often staying with various friends and caregivers to accommodate my parents' shift work. From kindergarten onward I was, to put it mildly, a headstrong headache to my teachers and the occasional truant officer. To everyone's relief, I spent summers with Grandmother until I learned how to drive—and to think of things beyond high school.

One of the less pleasant aspects during my childhood was the periodic booster shot. It was downright painful, much more so than today, especially to a headstrong young rebel like me. Today I'm a strong proponent of vaccines, especially when they're administered competently and with less pain that I recall from childhood. As I vaguely knew then—and as I know now for sure—they're for my own good and the good of those around me. But back then, as an ornery kid, I just *hated* them.

Grandmother's solution was typical of her dual role as magician and diplomat. Our doctor's office was right next to the local Ben Franklin, a five-and-dime variety store. (This particular Ben Franklin was owned by Sam Walton of later Walmart fame.) It was a truly magical place, full of fun and fantastic things to fuel a child's imagination. Grandmother made it an event, finding me a particularly wonderful item and taking obvious delight in my happiness. But the back door of Ben Franklin's led straight to the clinic! Almost without realizing it, I found myself at the doctor's, waiting for the dreaded booster shot. Checkmate.

Unpleasant as the latter still was, you may wonder why I continued to be fooled by our trips to Ben Franklin. You may also doubt my grandmother's integrity, imagining her to be engaging in some Pavlovian scheme. Nothing could be further from the truth. This was true leadership.

I soon figured out the routine, but I also did something more important. I mentally *assessed* where we were and what it meant—not just the momentary delight and pain, but also the things less easy to identify. I knew that her tough love was really unconditional, and that she always had my back. Even though I was an obstinate child, my mindset began to shift. I began to identify more profoundly with Grandmother's cleverness and insight, and knew I wanted to be more like her. Maybe most importantly, I began to think less about where I was at the moment and more about what could be next.

So, before we begin, let's review the basic principles I learned from my larger-than-life grandmother, as she raised me in my early years:

- I had the freedom to make my own choices, even when it was beyond my experience level.
- I learned to be self-sufficient, to overcome my fear of the unknown, and to move forward in the face of adversity.
- I learned what it means to work hard to provide for myself and the needs of my loved ones, and also that anything can be negotiated.
- I experienced motivation and reward that early on made me value work.
- I overcame basic fears led by my fearless grandmother, but she also taught me to be aware of threats and real danger.
- I took on new tasks where I had to learn unknown skills and become a valued contributor to the family.
- I learned to be curious and solve problems. On the farm, it isn't easy to just call a repairman. But there were other times when we needed someone especially skilled or with the right equipment to fix something, so having good relationships with those people were important too. I learned that leadership was key to any enterprise, from running a farm to getting a kid a vaccine.

These lessons formed a mindset that I believe influenced the rest of my life. From all this, I hope you can imagine something of my journey—literally from an outhouse to a penthouse—as a model for growth, change, and ultimately as a measure of success. As we walk through the what and the how of these growth cycles, I will recount similar experiences and events (and some other remarkable people) that have blessed me over the last few decades. This is part of my way of describing a process that has benefitted my career. I hope it benefits yours as well.

A Guide to GAIN

> The world is our platform to mean something.
> —**Stefan Pruett (Peachcake)**

When I set out to examine my own path in detail, I discovered a clear rhythm of cycles that spanned my entire career and tended to span approximately six or seven years each. Within each of these cycles existed a clear set of actions that turned up over and over again. Four of these actions became the concept of the Gain Principle: Go, Assess, Identify, and Next. I have done my best to truthfully discover how I managed to make it from the outhouse to the penthouse and honestly portray how I think you can use GAIN to help you on your way. As I wrote this book, I often wondered how much more success I might have found if I had identified these cycles early in my career instead of just intuitively going down the path.

This book is divided into two parts. The first is a description of what I've come to describe as *growth cycles*—those predictable patterns that define the beginnings, the middles, the presumptive ends, and the reboots (or rebirths) that most of us experience throughout our lives. The second part will focus on the how aspects of these cycles, particularly how to recognize them earlier, take advantage of opportunities sooner, recognize and overcome barriers, and ultimately make each cycle shorter, avoiding the mistakes we all tend to make along the way.

Some of the chapters in this book involve concepts that can be applied throughout a growth cycle. One of these critical components is what I call *leapfrog moments*, those unexplainable flashes of insight that shift your mindset and move you in new and unexpected directions. When I say "unexplainable," I'm not being entirely honest. After all, this book is my attempt at explaining them. Of course it's impossible to fully know the neurological or spiritual source of these insights, but I will try to explain—through my own experience and others'—my ideas on what these insights are and how to recognize them.

Other chapters will also deal with concepts that apply throughout a growth cycle. Among these is the need to learn from one's failures and the corresponding need for courage and resilience. In my own life, even when I began to understand how growth involved cycles, or when I trusted my own abilities and the support of others, progress to the next step was never automatic; I had to find in myself the courage to take the next step. As a child, merely knowing that Grandmother had my back—or my backside—did not take away my fear or keep me from making mistakes. With her help, I had to summon the courage, actually *do* something, make mistakes, and remember to learn from them. The same is true for adults.

The chapters in Part 2 will delve into the practical aspects of recognizing and benefitting from our own growth cycles. First of all, each person's patterns of growth are different. A cycle you experienced early in your career will look very different from what you're experiencing now. But there are similarities that are well worth knowing. There are definite advantages to recognizing these similarities and learning from them. There are also pitfalls to avoid. The first of these is the mistake many of us make when we first notice a pattern of any kind. Humans love it when they see a neat and tidy pattern to things. It's comforting. But that can lead to becoming complacent and not looking out for unexpected obstacles or dangers. Also, just because you recognize a pattern in your own growth cycles does not guarantee success. You still must actually *do* something about it.

Lastly, in Part 2 we'll talk about the nature and value of those around us who make benefitting from growth cycles possible. In my own case, Grandmother was the first of many people I've been blessed to know—*actual* influencers, not social media influencers—who helped me see what growth cycles were and, more importantly, how to take the next step, the one after that, and so on.

At times, I think I may be a slow learner. I suspect we all are when it comes to growth and change. Eventually, and with the help of those we trust, we all can take steps and shorten each cycle as we learn. My reason for writing is fueled in part by my desire to become such an influencer for you.

The principles in this book are not magic formulas or quick fixes for you to memorize. Rather, they are guideposts that I wish I had seen more clearly at the time. Looking back, after decades of trial and error, it seems easy to point these out. However that may be, it's my hope that the lessons I've learned, the people I've encountered, and the principles these pages describe will help you answer the question, "How can I do likewise?"

You will notice that at the beginning of each chapter, there is a song lyric or quote, sometimes from a famous artist, sometimes from my son Stefan, and sometimes there is a saying from me. All of these come from a time in my career where I was deeply impacted by what I heard.

A word about my son: Stefan Pruett was an accomplished musician and lyricist who was known the world over for part of his career as "Peachcake" and for the last part of his career as "The Guidance." He toured the world spreading a message of peace, love, and understanding, and also personal accountability for taking actions to lead yourself to your dream. What he wrote about and performed was way ahead of his time. He was a true believer in the value of the common person and equal rights for everyone.

The components of a growth cycle will be spelled out in greater detail in Chapter 1, but a brief overview is in order here. Every growth cycle has four basic parts:

GO —For many growth cycles, especially the early ones, this is the step involving the least amount of introspection and perhaps the greatest amount of *courage*. Simply put, it means going for something that has captured your imagination with everything you've got. My first GO moment chasing Grandmother was impulsive and headstrong, as you would expect from a three-year-old, but successive GO moments have become a tad more rational. Yours will too, if you choose to act. Of course, the GO phase benefits greatly from knowledge and insights gained during previous cycles, and from the wisdom and encouragement of our trusted influencers. In order to advance, sometimes you just have to GO. After you make that first move, the next step in the cycle is to ...

ASSESS—A certain amount of feedback and assessment happens almost immediately when you begin a cycle. This feedback and assessment comes typically from colleagues and managers as part of the normal flow of work in a new situation. If you're smart, you'll internalize this information—both good and bad—and adjust your performance accordingly. But the ASSESS stage happens when you take stock personally of where you've landed and where you're going—under existing conditions.

Assessment also involves study of what you are doing now and want to do in the future, plus developing the skills to get there. It's also known as "due diligence" in the financial world. This is nearly identical to how you develop a business plan.

In my experience, this step of intensive self-assessment occurs around the third year or so of a cycle, but actual timing varies for each individual. This assessment isn't a one-and-done event. It continues for two or three years—again in my personal experience—and never entirely goes away throughout the cycle. It involves consciously applying new habits and reinforcing existing ones, while periodically taking stock of the results and their implications.

Realizations from early ASSESS stages led me to leapfrog moments even in my earliest jobs. By assessing what was going on at the place I worked, I saw ways I could develop a path to the top.

From my sales jobs I realized that TV stations were driven by advertising. In those days, it was 100 percent of the revenue so I strived to learn everything I could about local advertisers' needs, determined how we handled the execution of advertising. As a salesperson I had access to every aspect of the execution, which also allowed me to know how the station worked overall. This learning and asking questions became a discipline that served me well as an investment banker and owner of TV stations.

From reading books about entrepreneurship and finance, I realized that businesses were driven by profit, so I set out to shift my thinking from employee to businessman, which is when I learned that everything started from a business plan.

Naturally, the results of the ASSESS stage will benefit your current situation. If done well, it will also benefit the situations of those around you. Eventually, however, the period of incremental assessment and improvement will lead you to the next step in the cycle, which is to . . .

IDENTIFY—This is when a significant mindset shift occurs. In my own experience, it tends to happen right around year four in a given cycle. It may be completely logical and rational in hindsight, or it may be a totally novel idea—a leapfrog moment. Essentially, this is the moment when the idea for your next growth cycle begins. At the time, this initial identification may only be a small piece of the picture, with details to follow. But the moment itself is the planting of a seed. The phase itself involves clarifying the next cycle—giving it roots and branches, so to speak—again preferably with the help of a trusted influencer. But an important aspect of this phase is that it should not detract from your current position or work quality. If anything, clearly identifying the next cycle can enhance the context and quality of that work. Then, sometime after the IDENTIFY stage has had room to develop, the fourth stage of one's growth cycle typically begins, which is . . .

NEXT—As the word indicates, this stage is where the details for acting on your new insight begin to take shape. In my experience, this tends to happen around year five, but it's difficult to pin down exactly. It definitely does not mean making sudden "escape plans" or neglecting your current responsibilities. It does not mean abandoning others by leaving a position without warning. In fact, a thoughtful and well-executed NEXT phase will likely improve your current work profile and prepare those around you for better outcomes in the future. Naturally, it is less than ideal to publicly announce that you're planning the NEXT phase. Rather, this phase is best executed in concert (and with the help of) with your trusted influencers and allies. As Chapter 1 will explore, not everyone will be okay with your move to the next cycle, but doing so anyway requires, and in many cases fosters, a greater measure of courage. Keep in mind that a NEXT is the last position before a new GO.

It's important to remember that a formula by itself is no substitute for the real thing. As I hope these pages will prove, considering and acting upon each of these stages is far more powerful than being able to recite a formula, a list of steps, or a PowerPoint slide from a business book.

Finally, as I hope to make clear in the coming pages, the growth cycles I have discovered for myself can be different in degree but not in essence from those you experience. They can be longer or shorter than mine. They do not necessarily mean moving to a different job or company, as mine have. You may well stay with the same company or association for decades while also experiencing and benefitting from the effective use of growth cycles. Ultimately, whether your growth cycles involve job or career changes, exponential improvement within the same job, or some other increase in effectiveness and satisfaction, my hope remains the same.

While I wrote this book with careers in mind, the Gain Principle can be used for almost any development project, business or personal. The cycles can be as long or short as you need them to be to suit a specific purpose. For that matter, even your career cycles within reason can be shorter than mine. My cycles came about from me looking back over a decades-long career and analyzing my behavior over that time. At the time, I was completely unaware of the cycles. I was busy doing things, or at least trying to do things.

My reason for writing this book is the hope that your own personal growth cycles will become increasingly obvious, welcome, and useful in reaching the next big thing in your life.

Exercise for the Reader

Each chapter of the book will conclude with a proposed exercise for the reader—one designed to help you internalize the concepts I have found to be so helpful over the years. (Rest assured, there will not be a test.)

For each exercise, I recommend that you take a clean sheet of paper, or a notebook or journal, to record your responses, insights, or stray thoughts on the subject. (I have no objection to your making notes on a digital device, but I've found that handwritten notes create a better, longer-lasting impact.)

For this introduction, let's start with some basic exercises:

1. Write down the names of people who have been influencers—the real kind—in your life and work. These can be family members, teachers, colleagues, or just about anyone who has moved you to GO, ASSESS, IDENTIFY, and proceed to NEXT. (If you wish, jot down your favorite account of an interaction with that person that proved to be a milestone.)
2. Pick something from your past that qualifies as a monster—something to be feared and avoided if at all possible. Write down as many details as you like, including how you hopefully overcame it. This book is not intended as therapy (nor am I in any way a qualified therapist), but I've always found it helpful to recall something big and scary that I've overcome to any degree.
3. Recall and write down an incident from your own life or work that proved to be much more significant and beneficial in hindsight than it seemed at the time. Write down as many details as you wish, and don't worry about writing style. (Remember, there will not be a test.)
4. Identify a GO moment in your own life and look at it analytically.

A last piece of advice: leave plenty of room below each entry or in the margins to allow for more notes and insights as you continue to read and absorb these ideas.

Wherever your individual growth cycles may lead, I wish you only the very best.

PART ONE

INTRODUCING GROWTH CYCLES

Chapter 1

The GAIN Model for Growth

All you need is a computer and a little belief in yourself.
—**Stefan Pruett (Peachcake)**

To be clear, it all starts when you start. Lessons I learned decades ago as a desk worker and then as a street seller formed the way I approached business in much the way my grandmother formed my approach to life. Pursuing direct rewards, tenacity, drive, and resilience, I learned in spades as a salesperson. I also used my position to learn the company's business model and how it functioned, which came in handy later when I learned about business plans. When I was learning the business as a salesperson, it was primarily so I could be a more effective seller—it eventually made me an effective entrepreneur and executive.

In spite of life's roadblocks (or maybe because of them), I maintain that growth is always possible, even for those laboring under disadvantages.

This isn't a pie-in-the-sky theory. All of life is cyclical, from organic life to the seasons to relationships to whole societies. Popular culture is loaded with it. All the major religions and philosophies are inhabited by some version of birth, life, death, and rebirth. So, even though I have been slow at times in recognizing these cycles in my personal and business life, the idea still rings true. The more I apply these ideas to my own life, the shorter and more efficient these cycles become.

My own appreciation for growth cycles did not occur early in my career. I wish it had. Like most of us, it was a seemingly random chain of opportunities—seized upon or missed spectacularly as chance would have it. I was fortunate enough to have an emerging passion for media and broadcasting. But passion alone is not enough. The cycles and process that I realized existed from analyzing my own career will help you smooth out the journey and make better decisions.

Just to be clear, not everyone starts with a specific passion for a particular field or a specific journey. Many adolescents and not a few grown-ups struggle to find a meaningful vision for anything. Some must discover it along the way or change their focus in the light of new circumstances. Too many are under unfair circumstances that squelch and discourage even the best of us. Many I have met see new opportunities for the first time and experience moments of edge-of-the-cliff panic. Frankly, so do I. You have to move past that fear and make a desire to achieve your ally.

From an early age, I've been captivated by broadcasting, particularly radio and television. Their enormous power to inform and influence others was awe-inspiring to me as a young man—as it still is today. The more I learned about how broadcasting involved real people and real jobs, the more I wanted to be part of it.

Then I learned it was possible for someone to *own* a radio station. It was like finding out that the Wizard of Oz was really a man behind the curtain, and that someone like me could become Oz, the Great and Powerful. Like the three-year-old me chasing Grandmother's 1954 Studebaker, I wanted to go for it, by any means necessary . . . even though I had no idea how.

Shortly after graduating from high school, I landed my first "plum job," the midnight-to-six shift at KSHE radio, an up-and-coming progressive rock station located behind a drive-in in the suburbs of St. Louis. I was in hog heaven.

I had also started college at Southern Illinois University Edwardsville (SIUE), and I was thrilled that my initial college advisor allowed me to do whatever I pleased with my course schedule. I wanted to finish my degree as soon as possible, so I plowed through as many basic radio and TV (RTV) courses as I could find. But in doing so I also neglected to take about eighteen months' worth of basic studies—or "BS" as I tended to call them. Everything changed suddenly in my junior year, when my mentor went on sabbatical and SIUE's no-nonsense head of the radio and TV program became my new counselor.

He was disturbed by my headstrong breach of university protocol. In no uncertain terms, he said I would not be allowed to take advanced RTV courses, much less graduate, unless I completed the basic studies. Without forethought, I blurted something to the effect of, "Well, if you knew anything about the radio business, you'd have a job in the industry instead of teaching about it." With a slight grin, he leaned forward and said, "Young man, let me remind you that for you to graduate, I have to sign your diploma." Oops. There is a lesson here: "Know who you are speaking to before you say something they cannot unhear."

In hindsight, I should have taken a page from Grandmother's book of diplomacy, at least regarding my ill-advised jab. At most, I should have considered the wisdom of a well-balanced education. The damage had been done, however, and I had just ended (temporarily*) my stay in higher education. But those few minutes' confrontation had an even more profound impact on my career. With little chance of repairing the damage, I began to assess my real situation—a process that led to greater things than I could have imagined.

In retrospect, over the course of my career, I can see four principles or phases of what I call *growth cycles*, even though I was clueless about them at the time. Neither the cycle itself nor any of its stages are inevitable. Their total duration (about seven years in my case) will vary considerably for each person. But I am convinced that our personal and professional lives are marked by a rhythm, a pulse, whose pattern can be predicted with accuracy. If we anticipate and learn from each phase in the cycle, we can benefit from

---

* I was able to earn my MBA several years later, despite my lack of an undergraduate degree. Although that scenario is rarer today, I'm thankful it was still possible in the 1980s.

them—achieving satisfying results much sooner than we would by leaving our success to chance. Since I don't have as many sevens left as I once did, my own goal is to make my own growth cycles less than seven years.

As I will try to make clear throughout the book, going through a new cycle does not require moving to a new job with a new company, although it has for me. One may experience many growth cycles while remaining with the same company for years. The point is that each cycle changes *you*, no matter where you wind up at the end of the day.

The GO Phase

The beginning of every growth cycle is marked by the single-minded pursuit of the "one thing" that has completely captured your imagination. It may be a natural outgrowth of a previous cycle, or it may involve a critical leapfrog moment to an unusual or unexpected destination, as we'll see in Chapter 2. To many of those around you, such a pursuit may seem foolhardy or unwise. (Early in your career, it may actually *be* foolhardy and unwise, but we'll talk about learning from failure later in the book.) But the main thing to remember is that the GO phase must have the required daily allowance of audacity. Being timid or prone to second-guessing is not part of the program.

As you've probably guessed by now, I am a naturally headstrong, willful person. Many who know me would agree, with varying amounts of frustration. Running headlong down a country road at age three did not mark me as a wallflower. Neither did sending an outlandish business plan to my boss—one that to outward appearances had nothing to do with my sales position.

It's true, I was audacious. But audacity can take many forms; not all of them are as demonstrative as mine. No matter whether you are extroverted, introverted, or something in between, you can still be audacious and single-minded in your pursuit of that "one thing." In fact, a shy person, or someone who deliberately avoids acclaim for their actions, may have some advantages when it comes to the GO phase of the cycle. They are pursuing something solely for its own sake.

This phase may be helped or hindered by your individual personality. For example, if you are naturally optimistic and adventurous, your GO moments potentially may become random and undisciplined. If you're the calm, analytical type, you may take longer than necessary to GO. (But once you do, you're more likely to have assessed the move thoroughly.) Or if you're naturally forceful, passionate, or goal-oriented, you are more likely to GO in a new direction promptly—but you can sometimes be less sympathetic toward those who hesitate.

All this is to say that the initial, vigorous pursuit of something may seem obvious to some and intimidating to others. However, I maintain it is something entirely possible for everyone, no matter how you or others may feel about it. The popular idioms "go for it" and Just Do It™ (as my attorneys prefer that I phrase it) simply mean pursuing something in the face of doubt or trepidation, not pretending that those doubts don't exist.

Sometimes a GO moment is driven by the desire to get away from a trying or unpleasant situation. Early in your life, it can simply be a move that allows you to assess an opportunity more clearly. This can be hard to discern with clarity, so, if at all possible, always assess your *motivation* for making a GO move.

An important aspect of the GO phase is that it can happen at any point in the cycle, not just at the beginning. This will be disappointing to readers looking for a neat, four-step generalization,* but it is very much the case. In fact, later in the book, we'll find that there are often "mini-cycles" within a general growth cycle, whether it's your experience—like advancing your own career—or that of the team you're trying to manage.

One of the sure telltale signs of a GO decision is the feeling of sheer terror it can produce. You may have all the passion in the world about a new direction, plus the rock-bottom conviction that this is the direction you want to go. But once it becomes reality—something you are actually going to *do*, not just think about—a natural feeling of fear rises up. That feeling served our prehistoric ancestors well, saving them from being eaten or otherwise prevented from becoming our ancestors. But today, that primal reaction more often leads to missed opportunity.

There are many reasons why our brains use fear to try to "protect" us, even though they're clearly overreacting. We may be giving too much weight to others' opinions, or to the fact that others just don't have the same aspirations as we do. Let's face it, our "herd instinct" makes it hard not to conform. Or we may not believe we're smart or capable enough, or otherwise lack the means to take that kind of action. We may think we're too late—or too early. We may have failed once or many times before. Above all, we may be afraid

---

* I'm not saying that handy four-step formulas are a bad thing. In fact, they help us remember the important stuff. It's just that we tend to overgeneralize at times when we should be thinking things through more carefully. As Mark Twain once said, "All generalizations are false, including this one."

of what others may say or think (or of what we may say to ourselves) if our audacious plan fails.

However you deal with those fears, always realize that they are *symptoms* of something—namely that a GO decision has emerged, either from your own thoughts and aspirations or from those you've learned to know and trust. Remember that courage does *not* mean the absence of physical fear—the normal, pit-in-the-stomach feeling that keeps you up at night. It means acting in the face of that feeling, knowing there are risks as well as rewards that can occur only after you act on that inner voice.

As we'll explore later on, a GO phase may be the result of an unexpected leapfrog moment, or simply the NEXT phase of the previous cycle. But very often it comes about through sheer persistence, an unwillingness to accept the finality of a previous failure. I have been privileged to know several people who embody the latter, and whose persistence has encouraged my own.

Although essential, GO is not an end in itself. One can pursue endless threads with abandon, but without taking the steps that follow, you risk merely being seen as impulsive. Each decision to GO must be followed by a curiosity and determination to see what logically follows.

Profile: Mark Burnett and Phil McGraw

The idea for the GO phase of a growth cycle came to me as I was thinking about successful people I have encountered, and gotten to know well, in my media sojourning.

In particular, two "go-getters" stand out, television producer Mark Burnett and producer/talk show host Phil McGraw—"Doctor Phil" to many. Their rise to the top of their fields is both intriguing and informative. Their careers are marked not only by a repeated willingness to GO, but also by a relentless drive to follow up with ASSESS, IDENTIFY, and NEXT.

As I've worked with Mark and Phil over the years, I've gotten to know something about their early days. Neither one set out to become "media moguls" or even television producers. To escape from a blue-collar existence, Mark joined the British Army and went on to become a special forces operative. Phil played football in college (among other things, of course) and eventually became a psychologist. The leaps that lead them to the endeavors they're known for today are remarkable. But, as they themselves would tell you, such leaps are possible for others.

After the service, Mark simply kept moving forward. A friend convinced him to come to the US, where he took a job as a nanny/bodyguard in Beverly Hills. There, he also built a T-shirt business in (where else?) Venice Beach. His passion for endurance and the outdoors, springing from his time in the service, led him to compete in extreme adventure competitions. It was during those that he came up with the idea of creating a video presentation of the grueling Eco Challenge race and getting it distributed on cable. Pursuing that idea led him to identify something very new. A long, grueling event was difficult to package for public consumption, so he formed a plan to break it up into one-hour segments, something that led to the successful phenomenon we now know as *Survivor*. That success led him to gain further insights into television audience behavior, and to the creation of multiple successful shows.

Phil actually worked for years building a large psychology practice before playing the part on TV. He had also made a name for himself as a jury selection consultant, something that requires formidable powers of observation. Television was never part of his original plan, but a serendipitous and influential client by the name of Oprah Winfrey opened the door, and he decided to GO. After he began appearing as a guest on her show, the rest, as they say, is history. Since then, Phil has relentlessly pursued each new opportunity and persuaded many others to do the same. In meetings I have witnessed, Phil's passion and intensity dominate the room. Those he has had occasion to confront, out of genuine concern for them, typically thank him at the end of the meeting for providing meaningful and often GO-producing insights.

Both of these people started their own journeys simply by pursuing a passion for action. They both moved forward, taking steps without really knowing where they might lead. In the face of whatever fears they may have had, they both have made growth cycles a consistent habit.

In the next chapter, I will talk about the leapfrog moments for both Phil and Mark that separated them from all other TV producers and businessmen.

The ASSESS Phase

Taking stock of where you've landed and where you're going usually begins immediately after the GO phase, but typically peaks around the third or fourth year of a seven-year cycle. It's the time where you get to know and begin to work within existing conditions, become more proficient with your own skill set, and master new, sometimes unanticipated skills. This peak can be sooner or later depending on the industry, culture, and mindset of the people around you.

This can be the most personally satisfying aspect of a growth cycle. You are actively getting ahold of something you really *like* to do and are making measurable progress with it. You become preoccupied (or obsessed more likely) as you absorb everything there is to know about your current path. You want to "eat it for breakfast," as the saying goes. At the peak of the assessment phase, as you look at the progress you've made, you'll begin to think about going to a new level or applying what you've learned here to another passion or interest. What that may be is usually not clear right away, but it's often a symptom of what I call an *inflection point*. These can occur throughout a growth cycle, but they tend to first appear as you assess your progress.

An inflection point is not always the result of positive experience. It can also come from *not* experiencing success or from becoming weary from the resistance to your passion-fueled goal. For example, my first passion was music and radio production, but I wasn't getting very far with it. And as the graveyard shift disk jockey at KSHE, I didn't make nearly enough money to make a career. The notion of shifting to sales first came to my attention as I hung out with the station's salespeople. They seemed to have the greatest flexibility and highest income of all the employees at the station. The realization was beginning to dawn on me that I wasn't making it in the producer-talent role.

My inflection point happened with a chance meeting at an industry function, in a conversation with Hal Protter, a rising star in the industry. At the time, he was the youngest general manager of a major market television station in the country. In the course of our conversation, he simply asked if I'd ever thought about going into sales, something for which he thought I'd be well suited. This led to more discussion and eventually to my getting hired as a salesperson. This led to a new passion—helping advertisers make more money through the creative use of television advertising.

Hal remained a friend and was a major influencer on my career for more than thirty years. Long-term influencers you meet early in your career often help accelerate your growth as they succeed on their own paths.

By now, you're getting the idea that growth cycles are not always tidy and regular. In the midst of my assessment phase at KSHE (at the same time my college career was careening along), I experienced an inflection point of sufficient power to start a new "mini-cycle," setting me off on a new GO phase. Becoming a seller ultimately became a key success pillar in my career. The following story is the first time I put together the elements of GAIN in a mini-cycle that included a leapfrog.

How an Entry-Level Sales Job Let Me Learn the Entire Business

Upon leaving SIUE, *sans* degree, I took some starter jobs in radio and TV. I was eventually lucky to land a sales job at KPLR TV in St. Louis. It was nowhere close to my Wizard of Oz aspirations, but I was at least in my chosen industry. It was also a time to take my self-assessment process seriously, take stock of where I had landed (and why), consider where I was going, and look seriously at *existing* conditions, not at conditions as I imagined them. It was a series of eye-openers, including one that changed my trajectory entirely.

Having always taken my cue from books, I read voraciously on topics related to business and entrepreneurship. One of these, *The Entrepreneur's Manual* by Richard White, created a seismic event in my head—a mindset shift the effects of which remain with me to this day. I didn't know anything about high finance, much less about what it takes to fund a new venture, but White and other authors flipped a switch inside me. Using critical advice based on real-world experience, White convinced me that it was possible to design and manage a successful business model—even to the extent of funding that business. I had been captured.

Having identified my next big thing, I of course thought of making it happen in my own beloved industry. I had moved on from my sales position at KPLR and was working for a national ad rep firm. Nevertheless, I somehow managed to get a proposal in front of the company's owner and CEO, Gary Scollard. My proposal was audacious, to say the least. The business plan (my first) was to raise funds to obtain an FCC license and create a new TV station in Little Rock, Arkansas—for which I would garner a modest 5 percent ownership in the station.

This effort contained an education in three critical areas. I learned

1. how to construct a financial analysis and business plan,
2. the value of actually writing the plan, and
3. that delivering an idea to a decision-maker offers the possibility of support.

Apparently, Gary found my audacity and entrepreneurial enthusiasm intriguing. After calling me in for a meeting, he sat me down with his accountants to vet the details of the plan. To my surprise and delight, he ultimately gave me the go-ahead, but asked me to keep it quiet within the company. It was not uncommon for others to have their own side projects, but this one stood out.

For the next few years, one of my challenges was to remain effective in my sales job while also working on my next big thing. For the most part, I succeeded. (I also learned later that my "secret" project was known by more than a few of my colleagues.) But when the time came, I made my move to start a consulting company and, with Gary's support, took my first step as a media mover. Over the years, creating a consulting firm or project became a device I have used with much success as a pivot or transition.

While this step didn't get me materially closer to owning a radio station, it showed me that I was able to take an idea and give it life. My next step of starting a consulting company did lead to radio station ownership, which then led to a much larger ownership of TV stations. What I had learned during my ASSESS stage prepared me for identifying and achieving my new Next.

Knowledge is the key to success during the assessment phase. It requires you to be open to any potential source of information, including the *people* in your chosen environment. Many have been in the space longer than you. They may take a dim view of your "zeal without knowledge." But however off-putting such people can be, always remember three things:

- However passionate you are about your GO move, it's more than likely that you did not invent it.
- Sometimes you may learn something from someone who's been there, especially if you've been paying attention.
- They may learn something from you, even if your GO move is unorthodox or unusual and decide to back your plan.

Apart from people, there are of course many other sources of knowledge to fuel your assessment phase. The question is how to *manage* all that information in order to make meaningful choices. These days, with the merging and melding of searchable text, media, and all kinds of structured and unstructured data, it's easy to flood your mind with so much data that real assessment becomes difficult. So let's look briefly at some of the sources of knowledge needed to support your assessment of the course you're on.

First and foremost, the most effective tool for fueling the ASSESS phase is reading. This includes articles, books, quotations, and even everyday things like memos and blurbs. Even books on seemingly unrelated subjects or people, real or fictional, will empower you during this phase.

Having been in the media business for decades, I know well the potential power and impact of video and audio, in both their traditional and digital forms. If well produced, they can be both informative and compelling, eliciting powerful, visceral responses. But in my experience, video and audio can only go so far in helping you create an assessment framework—a mental context for evaluating where you are and where you're going. Audio and video are invaluable support media, reinforcing and giving emotional context, but the primary source of knowledge during this period is almost always the written word. This includes not only reading what others have written, but also *writing down* your own thoughts as well as what you hear. Having said that, I am a voracious viewer of online video and audio, whether YouTube, TV shows, or podcasts, and I am always learning and having thoughts triggered as a result.

I'll explain. When you listen to the words and ideas of others, preferably those with *bona fide* expertise and wisdom, writing down the words helps establish that knowledge in your mind. During the act of writing, more of the brain becomes engaged, literally establishing new neural connections. According to neurobiologist Barry Gordon, writing literally does something in your brain. In a recent *Scientific American* article, he noted that this increased neural activity results in improved organizational skills (from sequencing your thoughts and ideas), a boost in problem-solving and reasoning, and the growth of your personal vocabulary.

Be a notetaker. Write down your thoughts and ideas daily and keep them handy. I use a simple system of a set of 8.5 x 11" pads that I tend to organize by broad subjects. Sometimes I have two and at times five or six. I regularly carry the idea list with me, and once I have several pages on a particular subject I tear those out and file them in working file folders. I have also used multi-subject notebooks. Of course, you can do this on your computer, but I have always found my handwritten notes to be a better working medium than a bunch of digital files.

When others do the writing, the benefits are similar. Reading, particularly of longer, well-constructed sequences, actually creates greater neural capacity and, according to research, "rewires" your brain, boosting both intelligence and empathy. It is not an inherent ability in humans, however. At birth, our brains are not equipped to translate letters into sounds. When we learn to read, we're using parts of the brain that have evolved to do other things. If all goes well, we go from recognizing sounds and their meanings to associating symbols with those sounds and progressing from there. By continuing to read, we build on that miraculous process, and continually sharpen our ability to assess our own situation.

The best sources of such foundational knowledge are books—both the fiction and nonfiction varieties. I'll admit, this may sound self-serving coming from someone writing a book. But the fact remains that, in my own experience, books have provided the context for every growth cycle, particularly during the ASSESS stages.

For most people, the ASSESS phase begins with a solid framework of knowledge about your current position and existing conditions. But that's not all. That knowledge must also be accompanied by conscious choices on your part—to consciously develop and apply new habits (and reinforce existing ones) that benefit your current situation (of course) and hopefully that of the people around you. As you do so, you'll begin to see ways your position could change and improve—or decide to take what seems like an entirely different direction. The boundary line is often blurred, but this is usually the beginning of the next phase.

The IDENTIFY Phase

Through my ASSESS phase and by taking the risk of disclosing my ideas to people who could enable them, I learned some very key things that led to my next important mindset shift, which was to become a businessman rather than just an employee doing a specific function. I wanted to build businesses and at minimum be a key shareholder if not the sole owner. Those businesses happened to be radio and TV stations.

At one point in my career, I was a financier—an investment banker, to be more precise—specializing in developing television station properties for other people. I found great satisfaction in the process of raising funds, securing the FCC licenses for and then buying what I felt were potentially successful stations. I made sure the right people were aboard, and then sold the stations when the time was right. Although I owned or held a stake in over twenty TV stations during that period, I never owned more than three of four at any one time. After all, I had shifted to investment banking as the result of learning how to finance my own projects. It was a way to expand my reach faster than I could have as a station owner—or so I believed at the time. (In hindsight, my decision probably ended up lowering my wealth-creation trajectory.) Had I focused on holding on to properties and fully developing them, I may have created more wealth for myself, but I have done just fine.

Naturally, I had been assessing my situation more or less continuously, with the help of trusted colleagues and of course constant reading. At one point, however, a major inflection point occurred. Looking back, I realize it was a combination of regulation, external economic conditions, changes in the tax law, and a realization on my part that I wanted to do something different—something even more personally satisfying. Being a financier had been great, and I had become quite adept at it, but I was watching others run with the ball. I realized I wanted to run these companies myself, not just set others up for success. I had *identified* my next step. (This phase, by the way, took fourteen years—or it may have been two sevens and I missed a road sign.)

The following story shows how one Identify moment led me back from failure to my biggest success.

The Long Cycle

Almost all my main business cycles lasted approximately six or seven years. For instance, I was working in sales for six years before I transitioned fully to being an entrepreneur financing, building, operating, and then selling off assets of TV stations. I did this for seven years until I transitioned completely to finance and investment banking for which I ran my own finance firm for six years. Then I bought a business and failed, which led to four years of regrouping and starting over. Eventually, I returned to investment banking and consulting to rebuild my net worth, which lasted six years.

Here I had yet another major mindset shift. More specifically, I wanted to build companies as partner and owner/operator as opposed to primarily being a facilitator. I had owned a few things along the way, but ownership for me had been mostly a by-product of my financing services. I had not been a true owner/operator per se.

At that point, I entered what I call the long cycle. This actually was the beginning of my most productive career development and financial success. It created the stepping stones for getting to where I am now. Keep in mind, for every step above I was already using the principles of GAIN in each phase, even though I didn't always realize it. When I look back over my entire career I can actually remember the points where I had certain mindset shifts after I assessed where I was in my career and identified where I wanted to go. GO, ASSESS, IDENTIFY, and NEXT were ingrained into my thinking since the very beginning of my work life.

The long cycle I am referring to started at the end of a cycle of consulting and financing on projects that had been pretty lucrative. But a lot of my energy was spent cleaning up a failed investment from the telecom crash of 2000. I had been an investor and on the board, but I had not been on the management team. That project was a driver of my next mindset shift: I wanted to find a company that was financially insolvent and become the CEO/shareholder who turned it around.

In late summer 2001, I found the perfect company: Communications Corp of America, a small but highly profitable operator of twenty-five television stations that had become over leveraged. ComCorp was owned by some former finance clients of mine and had become seriously overleveraged because of an expansion plan gone wrong. There was resistance at first, as the leadership thought they could solve it themselves. When 9/11 hit, the financing world changed overnight.

In January 2002, I got a call from the CEO, who said they needed to hire me to help sort out their debt issues. After a six-month engagement, they wanted me to become a partner and CFO. Four years later, I led the company through a bankruptcy reorganization and became CEO from 2006 until 2012, at which time the company was sold for a large gain. From mindset shift through the sale, this cycle lasted twelve years. Even though my position changed over time, the mindset was exactly the same for the duration of the cycle. I might even argue that this cycle was longer since I continued along a similar mindset for my next project. But that led to me becoming a c-suite executive in a large public company, COO of Sinclair Broadcasting, which was never my plan.

What is my takeaway from this long cycle? During its course, I continuously used the GAIN principles, but the NEXT was always available to me on the same platform. I certainly evolved as a leader and businessman and gained many new skills while building a reputation in the industry. My biggest takeaway is that once you find a platform that will feed your GAIN needs, stay with it until it concludes, or until you cannot realize your GAIN there and need a new NEXT.

This is also the point where we talk about unintended consequences or outcomes. As a result of pursuing the status as company builder and operator, I ended up in the c-suite of a publicly held broadcaster, Sinclair Broadcast Group, because David Smith, the CEO and my original investor, wanted me to stay after my company merged with Sinclair. Financially and experientially, this worked out well for me, but I never intended to be a big company executive and probably wasn't particularly well suited for corporate lifestyle. I was too interested in change and doing new things.

The IDENTIFY phase flows naturally from ASSESS, although the cause and effect can be difficult to pin down narrowly. Sometimes it's an extension of your current interests and activities, while at other times it's a dramatic pivot in a new and unexpected direction. Regardless of which form it takes, this phase is marked by a fundamental *mindset shift*—an "Aha!" moment that makes complete sense in your current situation while at the same time pointing forward to what the next cycle will be.

In my own experience with this phase, I often don't know precisely what is going to happen or when. It is of course influenced by the specifics of previous stage, but it's not dependent on whether things are going well or not. If things are going poorly, the message is clear. We can learn from failure, as we'll discuss later in the book. In a crisis, you must take some sort of action to ameliorate a bad situation. But if things are going well, then the IDENTIFY phase will be more subtle. Absent a crisis, it takes time to collect all the details. This is why this phase can take up to two years. A savvy professional's thoughts will often turn to improving an existing situation, but the "lightning bolt" moments seldom happen all at once.

An interesting aspect of this phase is that it does not dictate the destination or terminus of your new direction—at least not immediately. In assessing where you are, you may find that your passions for your current situation have either waned or grown stronger, regardless of performance feedback. This is where identification becomes nuanced and somewhat controllable. You must listen to your inner self—but also question what that self is telling you. Identifying that inflection point becomes an almost spiritual trek, fed by reading, research, and periods of deep thinking, meditation, and/or prayer, if that's what works for you.

On the practical side, identification consists of a growing awareness of where your thoughts are headed in relation to the information you've acquired—from the ASSESS stage until the present moment. Previously, I stressed the importance of reading, particularly books, in setting off a train of thought, leading deeper into IDENTIFY. But I cannot exclude movies and television as valid sources of inspiration. Michael Tolkin's recent miniseries, *The Offer*, is a case in point. The docudrama is about "The Greatest Movie Almost Never Made" (namely *The Godfather*) and the harrowing experiences of producer Al Ruddy and his team while pursuing their artistic vision. Their persistence, in the face of constant rejection, derision, and even threats to their lives, directly impacted my thinking and created a construct for me in considering my next project.

For this phase, think of your sources of information and inspiration in two ways. Books, research, and other written materials are the bones and skin of your emerging idea. Movies, music, and other "ephemeral" media are the blood and breath that make it come alive. Both are needed to make the identification complete.

Finally, if you're having trouble envisioning the IDENTIFY stage in your own career, don't worry. As I said earlier, pivotal changes seldom emerge fully formed. However, you must be willing to *do the work*, namely investigate every available opportunity and set long-term and interim goals for the more promising leads.

A time-honored technique for goal setting in this case is to develop specific, measurable objectives that meet what's known as the "SMART" criteria:

- **S**PECIFIC – Are there real activities with tangible outcomes?
- **M**EASURABLE – Can we tell if something happened (or not)?
- **A**CHIEVEABLE – Can we really do it?
- **R**EALISTIC – Should we really do it?
- **T**IME-BOUND – When will we see and measure the results?

You may have to do this more than once, on your own behalf or in concert with your team. But with research, diligence, and no small amount of patience, the details of the IDENTIFY stage will become clear, and you'll be ready for the final stage of the growth cycle.

The NEXT Phase

Once you have experienced that *fundamental mindset shift*, and identified its essential details, you are ready for the final phase of a growth cycle. If you're in the tiny minority of people without too many pressing business obligations, it's possible—at least theoretically—to just head for the nearest exit. But for most people, the NEXT phase is a lot more complicated. It can take two or three years on average, not only to prepare yourself but also to make whole the people and processes you'll be leaving behind.

This doesn't necessarily mean that others have to feel good about it. If you're performing well in your current cycle, they won't be thrilled about the hole you're leaving. But feelings aside, it's vital in this stage to keep things running well, AND help make the transition as smooth as possible, AND prepare yourself for what will become your next GO phase. No pressure.

Another thing to remember is that this phase—and indeed life cycles in general—does not always mean taking a position with another company or embarking on an entirely new career path. Personally, I have taken some sharp turns over the years, or at least that's what it must look like to others. But it's possible to remain in the same line of work, or with the same company, and still experience your own powerful growth cycles.

The aptly named NEXT phase introduces a number of challenges ranging from business ethics and employee obligations to protecting the security of your income and the viability of your current position. Depending on where you are within an organization, this can mean different things.

For executives and senior managers, there are usually contractual obligations to owners and boards of directors that must be met. Within those constraints, the NEXT phase involves timely and constructive notice, as well as a realistic appraisal of practical matters, like vesting stock options. Even when a board is sympathetic, there are often legal obligations that take time to resolve.

If you are an employee, in middle management or otherwise, there is no rule about disclosing your desire to move on to something new. Having said that, however, there's an ethical obligation not to use company resources without permission to advance yourself outside the company. As a leader, I prefer that people tell me they want or need advancement and inquire if that is in the cards for them. For the employee this is a calculated risk, even if they do so with candor and diplomacy. Ideally, this will lead to honest discussions about their path, within the company or otherwise, without making false promises or creating false hopes. Sadly, in some companies the reaction might not be so constructive.

If raising your hand isn't an option, and you want to stay employed, then it's up to you to develop your NEXT strategy on your own time—and definitely *without* using company information, time, resources, or established customer relationships. Doing any of the latter will not only impede your progress but will also seriously damage your credibility and reputation—turning your NEXT phase into possibly your last.

During this phase, vacation and free time are the best opportunities to research, read, and make the necessary contacts. This applies to everyone, regardless of their position within an organization. In my early years in sales, I often made it known to my bosses that I spent lunch hours at the library or investigating unfamiliar aspects of the business. It was not always comfortable, but my rationale was that instead of long boozy lunches with clients I was focused on being the most informed salesperson my clients would ever meet. I would create value for them by being well informed. (Obviously, the library is no longer all you need today, but the principle remains the same.)

Life cycles can take many forms. After my early pivots, going from the music business to on-air broadcasting to sales and then to TV station owner, I found myself the CEO/founder of a company with three hundred employees. I decided I didn't have enough business education. Even though I had studied finance, accounting, and business planning independently, I longed to finish my formal education. This led to pursuing my MBA at the Kellogg School of Management at Northwestern University. While each cycle makes sense in hindsight, it may not be perfectly clear while it's happening. I do believe that getting an MBA from a top business school was a differentiator for me, so it was time and money well spent.

Like it or not, your career and your life are in constant development. You are either taking the lead or passively letting it happen. If you are leaning in and willing to change your mind, then your mind will begin to latch onto the next GO, the next ASSESS, the next IDENTIFY . . . and you'll surely begin to experience the thrill (and the stress) of what comes NEXT.

The cycle may involve a new business idea or a new area you would like to work in. It may be a logical transition to a specialty within your own sphere. But regardless of the form it takes, a growth cycle is pure opportunity. The more you recognize the steps and master them, the shorter each cycle will become, making your journey a memorable one.

Exercise for the Reader

While reading this chapter, you may have recalled episodes in your own business or personal life that have had a recurring, cyclical nature. It is useful to use your own past to judge the validity of the GAIN model.

Take a piece of paper and write down a particular time in your career. It doesn't matter if there's not an exact correlation to the four stages I've outlined, but it's always helpful to ask questions.

1. What was the "one thing" that inspired you to go forward and give it everything you've got?
2. How did you learn the ropes and develop new skills in your new pursuit?
3. Was there a mindset shift or inflection point—where you identified something logical but quantitatively different from your current path?
4. How did you prepare for the next move, to fulfill that new direction without jeopardizing the current one?

BONUS QUESTION 1: During this process, did you learn anything that would have made any of these steps shorter or more efficient?

BONUS QUESTION 2: Who was (or is) your key influencer during this particular cycle?

Chapter 2

Looking for Leapfrog Moments

We want what we want, but we don't know how to get it, get it
We think that we know what we want, but we won't ever get it, get it
We can't deny it, I will do it a new way
If we can destroy it, I will do it a new way
—**Stefan Pruett (The Guidance), "Subtext Destroyer"**

Leapfrog moments are critical and hard to explain, but I came up with a sports analogy that I think almost everyone can identify with. A top NFL quarterback is badly injured during a key game midseason, and the only replacement is the recently drafted rookie with no in-game experience. He comes in and leads the team to victory and fares well in subsequent games. He just leapfrogged in his career, because the next year he is either going to get a massive raise or be recruited to start for another team, jumping several years in a sport that has a short career span. That is a classic leapfrog moment. Sometimes the opportunity doesn't work out and the rookie fails, but sometimes it creates a whole new career.

In the previous chapter, I laid out the four components of a growth cycle, whether the cycle applies to your career progress or to the way you function within the same business over time. My own growth cycles have occurred in the former realm, defining my history as a restless, entrepreneurial spirit. But I have observed the latter many times in those who remain in the same profession, and even the same organization, for their entire adult lives. The question is not which type you are. The real questions are about the mechanics of GAIN. How do you move from one stage to another? What is the *spark* that inspires and drives you to GO for the thing that has captured your imagination? What then moves you to ASSESS your situation, to wring out every possible drop of information and knowledge? What leads you to IDENTIFY a new and unexpected gem, and ultimately to prepare for the NEXT thing you've identified?

There are two very different but equally powerful answers to those questions, one positive and the other seemingly negative. We'll deal with the second one in the next chapter, but for now let's look at the positive one, the leapfrog moment. Such a moment can occur at any time in the growth cycle, but especially during the ASSESS and IDENTIFY stages. It can also *seem* to be negative if you have a thin-skinned attitude toward criticism, as we'll see in a moment. It is nearly always unexpected, although in hindsight you'll realize it made perfect sense. Boiled down to its essence, it's a powerful, compelling departure from your own personal status quo.

That said, leapfrog moments are not actually all that rare. Often in public settings, especially in politics, people lack the courage and diligence it takes to go against the status quo and accomplish something meaningful. But on a private, personal level, it's more common than you think. *Anyone* is capable of finding that unique spark, that unexpected direction, and many people take that path every day. The challenge is to recognize those leapfrog moments in the context of your current growth cycle.

In general, leapfrog moments are thoughts or opportunities that can fundamentally change a material outcome or the direction you are heading at a given moment. They can be a series of events, small or large, that align to form a significant potential for change. Or they can be sudden, seismic events—the dramatic mindset shifts described in the last chapter. They can come from your own thoughts and reflections, springing from your quest for more knowledge during the ASSESS phase. They can also come from outside yourself, from a trusted friend or colleague, or even from your boss. (Ironically, they can also come from your conflicts, personal failures, and dealings with adversaries, but we'll keep that paradox on hold until the next chapter.) They can be the result of accumulating greater responsibility, such as finding things that need to be done and just doing them, even when they're not strictly part of your job.

The one thing leapfrog moments are not is *incremental*. It may take you time to assemble the pieces, but the net effect is always immediate and disrupting. Gradual change and improvement aren't a bad thing, but a leapfrog moment is not that. It takes you beyond your current comfort zone or skill set range and dares you to go against the status quo. It does not guarantee success, but it does open a path you did not expect. In short, it leads you to IDENTIFY the next major growth cycle.

Leapfrog moments have another major attribute. They happen when you are being *objective* and *self-aware* about your situation, when you step back and look at things from the outside. That means seeing yourself and your work as they really are, not as a heroic tale with you in the starring role.

It's a lot harder to be objective than you imagine. You have to be willing to question your mental models, your habits, and your biases—a process that requires mental effort. But as Nobel laureate Daniel Kahneman pointed out in his best-selling book, *Thinking, Fast and Slow*, we humans are naturally predisposed to "cognitive ease"—things that feel familiar, feel true, and feel effortless. This makes it easy to ignore things about yourself and your situation that are painfully obvious to others. It makes us prone to biased thinking and cognitive errors about ourselves and our situation. But if you allow new thinking and new perspectives to get through the bubble, and take a moment to stand outside the norm, a leapfrog moment is not far behind.

The Entry-Level Experience

Remember, it all starts when you start. These lessons can stay with you a lifetime, even if they seem small or irrelevant. Early in my career, I encountered a number of my own leapfrog moments. The first occurred while in college, writing for a local music magazine that covered St. Louis area rock concerts. For an eighteen-year-old, going to clubs and concert halls, meeting with bands and promoters then writing about them was an interesting job—not to mention a lot of fun. It brought me into contact with bright, driven young people ranging from wealthy rock promoters to successful band managers and all the many people it takes to handle a large tour.

At one point, however, it dawned on me that this was about more than a fun gig. The light bulb went off. I decided right then that I wanted to be a part of the action, not just an onlooker. That's when I got a job at a local rock station, doing the late shift and helping out in the promotion department.

By the time I was twenty, I had held a number of positions, mostly freelance, that involved the music and entertainment business. They included working at the magazine, the radio station, and some odd jobs for a major promoter in Missouri. It was then, I realize now, that I was about to make my second leap. But first let's talk about how to recognize your leapfrog moment, whether it's the first one or simply the next one in the cycle.

Leapfrog moments can come at any time, but they typically happen while you're in the ASSESS stage of a growth cycle. As we discussed in the previous chapter, this involves a diligent examination of your conditions, paying attention to what others are saying and absorbing information from every source available. It also involves something very important: recognizing your own personal status quo, the comfort zone that a leapfrog moment will undo. Knowing that your current state is not the peak of perfection, and that you're not as special as you think you are, will help you recognize the moment when it comes.

For me, moving from entry-level management to sales laid the groundwork for a significant leapfrog moment. The job put me in contact with business leaders and executives—including my boss. It was a position where performance really mattered, so I went into ASSESS mode to learn everything I could. I wasn't all that calculating about my moves; I just began to drink from the fire hose of available information. I devoured articles from broadcast trade publications as well as magazines about business and finance. I dug into the competition for each of my clients—which of course they loved to hear about. I found that knowledge itself was a service that advertisers were hungry for.

In the process, I also found out that if you could really sell, then the people you work with would start addressing your demeanor, your dress, and your education. I was adept at convincing certain businesses to advertise on television. I piled up wins with auto body shops, lawnmower shops, appliance stores, and motorcycle dealers. I was pretty full of myself, but clueless about things outside my experience. The sales managers recognized my talent, but as I soon learned, they knew I was too rough around the edges to handle larger accounts.

What happened next was one of those vividly remembered, pivotal moments that influenced my future. One day, a hard-nosed sales manager from Brooklyn, Manny Brooks, called me into his office. Without fanfare or explanation, he sat me down and said, "You know what? You dress like s***, kid." Then he wrote me a personal check for $500 and told me to go buy three suits, shirts, ties, and a pair of lace-up shoes. (It was 1976, so $500 could buy a lot.)

People can make a difference through a direct action rather than building a long-term relationship, which can be impactful over the long haul.

Throughout my career there have been people who took action to help me or coach me, even if they used harsh words to do so. Although I didn't have a word for it at the time, I was fully in ASSESS mode when, quite literally, Manny made me an offer I couldn't refuse. He didn't mince words (clearly), but he also gave me the perfect incentive to do something outside my own personal bubble. I had the opportunity to be objective, to step back and look at my appearance from another perspective. My leapfrog moment occurred because instead of griping about his attitude or clinging to my success with lawnmower and motorcycle shops, I got a glimpse of how others saw me. (I wasn't too thrilled about it, by the way.) In a way, it was a mini–growth cycle all by itself, leading me to the next IDENTIFY and NEXT phases of my sales career.

For anyone at the beginning of their career, leapfrog moments are not easy to identify. You are inundated by information, sometimes engaging, sometimes boring, but always overwhelming. You have every reason to shut out unwelcome, uncomfortable thoughts. It's a perfectly normal, human response. But it will keep you from moving forward. On the other hand, if you let your ASSESS phase include interruptions to the status quo (which are chances to be objective) then you'll find unexpected benefits.

Stephen Covey defined self-awareness in *First Things First Every Day* as "our capacity to stand apart from ourselves and examine our thinking, our motives, our history, our scripts, our actions, and our habits and tendencies." He goes on to say that it comes from asking and answering hard questions. That is not a practice limited to young people just starting out, of course. I should know. Hard questions are a blessing, no matter when they appear. If taken seriously, they lead to moments that will accelerate your personal growth cycles.

Activating the Mindset Shift to Businessperson

To reiterate: leapfrog moments are not limited to the beginning of your career. They can and should occur later on—continually, in fact—whether you're moving from one organization to another (as I have) or transforming yourself and your trajectory within the same organization. The conditions and impacts of these moments are similar to those that happen in the beginning. However, with greater business experience often comes greater complexity and nuance. It is no longer sufficient to just "get your act together" personally, as I did under Manny Brooks's gentle admonition. Rather, you need to cut through the noise of everyday activity in order to change your position within an organization, to make that transformative break from the status quo.

To make that change, *a major mindset shift is required*. This was a defining moment for me when I began thinking like a businessman. In order to make a leapfrog move, try looking at your job not only from your boss's point of view but also from *their* boss's perspective or that of the business owners. For starters, ask yourself how well you know your company's strategy and business model. A big part of leapfrogging is to become more entrepreneurial—to think like an owner even before you become one. Whether you rise through the management ranks over time or you start your own business, thinking like a business owner will differentiate you from the rest of the pack. Or as Mike Kublin, the founder and leading development executive of Peopletek, once said, "First lead yourself, then lead others" (peopletekcoaching.com/2022/03/15/fly-then-lead-others).

Think of these moments as internal motivation, or "entrepreneurial aspirations," whether or not they lead you to start an actual new business. Sometimes they are driven by *opportunity*, that push to achieve greater autonomy, freedom, or mastery over something. In Daniel Pink's book, *Drive*, these are described as intrinsic motivations, which are vastly more powerful than the extrinsic motivations of financial reward. (That is not to say that leapfrog moments don't involve increased wealth. They often do.)

Such moments may also be driven by *necessity*. When facing the possibility of unemployment, financial reversal, or simply a loss of control, you'll be much more open to a leapfrog moment that can change your trajectory and lead to a new cycle of growth. As we'll see in the next chapter, there's nothing quite like a crisis to make you re-think your tried-and-true routine.

Here are a few examples of major leapfrog events (from some names you may recognize!):

- Dr. Phil McGraw—From jury consultant to TV host to owner/producer of TV shows
- Mark Burnett—From commando to event producer to TV producer to studio owner
- Steven Pruett—From TV ad sales to investment banker to small TV company CEO to public company c-suite

It does not matter whether a leapfrog moment presents itself as an opportunity or a matter of necessity, a push from within or a pull from outside circumstances. The important thing to remember is, when you recognize the moment for what it is, you must act on it. In the example that follows, Mark Burnett and Phil McGraw—who were both already successful leapfroggers—made massive leapfrog decisions after they were already accomplished in the careers they had created.

Profile Update

In the previous chapter, I noted two of my business associates, Mark Burnett and Phil McGraw, who have informed my ideas on growth cycles and who, in my opinion, demonstrate some of the most proactive aspects of GAIN. Both of these men have also had significant leapfrog moments, which, because they took full advantage, set them apart from typical businessmen or TV producers.

When Mark first pitched *Survivor* to CBS, he made a fateful and risky decision to forego much of his guaranteed fee. He also agreed to shoulder some of the show's financial risk. At the time, this practice was unheard of in the television industry. But it transformed and differentiated Mark from being a typical producer into an entrepreneurial media owner. His decision, coupled with his prodigious creativity, drive, and work ethic, put Mark Burnett in a class by himself.

Similarly, Phil followed the lead of his biggest influencer, Oprah Winfrey. Initially, she had owned his new TV show, but later, at her behest, he took the financial risk to buy out her interest and become the sole owner of the *Dr. Phil* show.

By recognizing and taking their respective leapfrog moments, both Phil and Mark became essentially independent television studios, transforming them into major powers in the television network and syndication landscape for over two decades.

For me, activating the mindset shift to businessperson was triggered by reading *Financier: The Biography of André Meyer* (someone once referred to him as "the Picasso of banking") as well as Richard White's *The Entrepreneur's Manual*, as I related in Chapter 1. The examples and stories about business owners who were also entrepreneurs fired my imagination and prompted me to want a business of my own. Since I was already in the media business, I decided to write a business plan for acquiring new television station licenses and building stations in markets that I knew (from my experience as a national sales rep) were inventory constrained.*

How did I figure out my first business plan for a TV station without having ever been a manager? I knew from the demand on existing stations that a new station would get a certain percentage of budgets just by default, in order to bring down market prices.

Prior to being a national rep, I had been a local ad salesman. (See the section in chapter 1 on how my first sales job prepared me to write a business plan.) So I figured out my plan by retracing my steps as a local station seller, tracing what had to happen from the time I made a sale to getting it on the air. I carefully noted each desk, office, and job title by recounting a process I had done many times. Thankfully, we were not automated or computerized in those days. Every step required human interaction, including people from programming, billing, and collections, and even getting approval from the general manager. I learned the business structure of the

---

* In those days, before the explosion of cable channels and the internet, a market with fewer TV stations had a limited number of available "slots" for advertisers. As companies demanded more time for their ads, the need for more stations increased.

Looking for Leapfrog Moments | 69

station by simple observation and recollection.

White's book had given me the format for a business proposal, to which I added details from William G. Droms's *Finance and Accounting for Non-Financial Managers* and a few insights of my own. That was "the book" to me, and it got me started in learning about corporate finance. When I presented my idea to the company president, he recognized its potential, despite (or maybe because of) my audacity, and helped me move it forward. My leapfrog moment was the culmination of several factors, but it only became a real moment of growth when I chose to act.

Professional and Personal Growth

As you progress through your career(s), you'll notice that your personal and professional growth cycles overlap and interact with each other. Sometimes, they may be somewhat out of sync. You may be deep in the ASSESS phase of a personal situation while simultaneously working on the NEXT phase of a new business opportunity. Because you're only human, one cycle can potentially wreak havoc on another. But, if you are mindful of the situation, one growth cycle can inform and enhance the other one. In fact, a leapfrog moment of realization in one area may lead to an unexpected resolution in another.

Being aware of these dynamics requires a certain level of psychological maturity. Just because you have identified the next big thing in your career or business does not automatically mean that others—even those with a big stake in the outcome—will see it as clearly as you do. It is something of an art to hold a newly discovered leapfrog moment in the forefront of your mind while also recognizing and respecting those who don't get it, and maybe never will. It's an art that some psychologists call *mindfulness*.

Without going into the philosophical side of things, mindfulness simply means being "in the moment," being aware of and paying attention to what is happening, to you personally, to those around you, and in particular to the phase of a growth cycle that you (and they) are in. Being self-aware and non-judgmental will lower the tensions in yourself and those around you. More than that, it will help calm the turmoil of everyday business (or "busyness," more accurately) and allow new thoughts or insights to emerge. Being mindful can smooth or even accelerate the progress of a growth cycle. It can help clarify why a particular person or situation is seemingly out of sync with others or with a business strategy. More importantly, it can also lead to brand-new, unexpected leapfrog moments.

Leapfrog Moments at the C-Suite Level

Finally, the occurrence of leapfrog moments does not cease as you move to higher positions of responsibility. If anything, they increase and become more complex—if you embrace them for what they are. When such a moment reveals an important facet of a growth cycle, it can potentially move everyone forward, and transcend the blockage of boardroom-level politics and maneuvering.

Good executives must be able to juggle multiple, detailed circumstances within a business. At the same time they must be effective in their appointed role, maintaining operational efficiency (the COO), technical innovation (the CTO), financial health (the CFO), or long-term vision (the CEO). With so much going on, recognizing and taking advantage of growth cycles can get lost in the shuffle. With so much at stake, executive-level leaders need to seize upon leapfrog moments as they appear, not to distract from their main purpose but to discover a new, often unexpected way to fulfill that purpose.

At the c-suite level, leapfrog moments (and GAIN growth cycles in general) can take on new meaning. Both require the absorption of multiple skills, perspectives, and mindsets. They can propel an individual to consider a different phase of their own career. But they can also transform the business itself or create an entirely new business where none existed previously. Very often, the leapfrog moment that had personal and professional significance for one individual will have a series of ripple effects for many others, causing them to GO in brand-new directions.

My first viable company was formed with a partner who raised funds for a limited partnership for the purpose of buying several small radio stations. Results of this fundraising experience triggered something in me. It was a leapfrog moment that would eventually lead me to building a much bigger company, one involving TV station ownership.

We were able to sell the assets for more than what we paid, which not only created a modest return but also identified something new. Our limited partnership had used tax advantages and market factors to finance and build new stations. It occurred to me that this model could be applied on a much larger scale!

The moment was followed by three confirming events. Soon afterward, I met with several businessmen who had TV licenses in major markets but no money. I then searched for and found a firm that would raise operating capital for the stations if we got them built. I located equipment manufacturers who would lend us 120 percent of the equipment costs because we had operating capital. As general partners, we took fees for management and financing plus 25 percent of the gain on equity. As general partner, I became the controlling party and licensee. It was a successful model, confirming the leapfrog moment I had recognized earlier. From 1981 to 1986, I did twenty-two of these deals for a total of approximately $200 million in funding. When leverage was applied, that $200 million in equity turned into $500 million of total investment power.

It was during this time that I developed the concept of leveraging equity partnerships with debt, which did not exist in the 1980s outside of very large corporations. By the mid-1980s, when the Reagan administration changed the tax laws and closed our easy equity path, we had a track record sufficient to raise money privately, without the tax advantage, and could make purchases on the economics of purchasing profitable stations with a small amount of equity and then borrowing on top of that.

Successful business people are always aware of the regulatory environment and its potential impact. At the time this happened, I was young and naïve. I didn't see it coming, but I managed to pivot. Building on this strategic, financial knowledge, this endeavor became the basis for a boutique investment bank, one that went on to finance more than a billion dollars in acquisitions by 1992, and for which I received fees and equity. (A billion dollars in the 1980s was a big number.)

As we worked our way through this series of financial deals, I became increasingly aware of the interplay between C-level decision makers. My leapfrog moment had a cascading effect, not only within my growing private equity firm, but also among the leaders of the stations we acquired and sold. Although I had not yet defined growth cycles as such, I was clearly accelerating through a major one, as were the executives impacted by each transaction. We had become aware of not only where we were but also what the next phase would be and how we would get there.

Not that this particular cycle was perfect. As with any business situation, we had great successes, some failures, and even disagreements that led to legal actions. In spite of those failures (which we'll explore in the next chapter), the net result of those leapfrog moves has been extraordinarily positive, mentally, physically, and economically, for me and for the majority of others involved.

Leap or Grind?

In the world of business, it's all too common for people to experience the slow, incremental process of rising through the ranks—what I call "the grind." What seemed like a promising start, a seeming GO moment, ended up being a mismatch between one's talents or passions and the actual job requirements. With little incentive to vigorously ASSESS and IDENTIFY the situation, promotion becomes a waiting game, a hope that a new position with higher pay will open up someday. In the meantime, people merely endure the disconnect between what they desire and what they're paid to do.*

One big problem with the grind is that it blinds us to how others perceive us and how we perceive the world around us. The results are habits that maintain the status quo rather than examine and challenge it. The opportunity to GAIN is stifled by a mindset of "that's the way we've always done things." But, as Marshall Goldsmith's excellent book title puts it, *What Got You Here Won't Get You There*, bad habits that seemed inconsequential early on will invariably hold you back from growth and fulfillment. Progression is possible

---

* The Great Resignation, amplified by the Covid-driven lockdown, has made it clear that people are more willing than ever to abandon these unfulfilling jobs and seek opportunities aligned with their talents and passions. For them, the potential benefits of embracing the GAIN model are staggering.

by grinding away, getting promoted layer by layer, but it's fraught with the risk of getting stuck in the middle, even if you're talented.

The alternative to the grind is the leap. Most of the leaders and executives I have known did not rise slowly or incrementally, or by doing what they've always done before. Like everyone else, they experienced frustration and pushback, not to mention criticism, but nevertheless found the opportunity to transcend the status quo and bypass the obstacles before them. In fact, many of the executives I have known got to where they are now via multiple leapfrog moments. From my own experience, I believe that anyone can do so and avoid the dismal path of simply grinding your way along. Even people who grind their way to the top experience leapfrog moments; otherwise, they become stuck in the middle.

Sadly, companies often suffer from inertia, and this applies to how they handle the advancement of talented employees. If you cannot advance your ideas where you are or the way things are done is blocking you, then you have no alternative but to seek someone outside the company or at least outside your direct sphere. Usually, an internal leapfrog takes place by grabbing a position people in better positions don't want. Here's a fictional example: Let's say you are a successful seller in a top division, but there are people in line above you to become sales manager of that division. When a senior sales manager job comes open in a weak division, no one wants it. This is a good opportunity to leapfrog because even in failure you will likely still be two rungs higher on the ladder. If you are successful, you might end up returning to the top position as the boss of others who declined it, plus now you are three rungs higher positioned for a division manager job.

Estimated time: two to three years. Time saved? Probably five years.

On the corporate side of things, I have observed several conditions that will help you be more likely to discover your own leapfrog moments (and less likely to accept the grind approach):

First, always perform at the highest level in your current position while also knowing what the other, adjoining positions entail. It's a situation similar to the NFL (or any professional sport, for that matter). Even an All-Pro running back has to win his position as a starter—and even to make the team—when training camp starts. It requires diligence to master your own moves and skills. But it also requires a solid working knowledge of every other position, both offensive and defensive. Supporting and being supported by others on your team, in sports and in business, requires you to know what everyone does when they're at their best.*

Second, always strive to understand the business model of your entire company. Use that understanding to build cross-functional relationships that benefit everyone, not only you or your division. This is something you can do while also doing your day job. Knowing the business model means knowing both strategy and function, and how these affect your responsibility. You can gather this information simply by looking at the functional roles of those around you, asking questions, and discovering the workflow that generates the best results. Things like inventory, sales, order processing, and delivery may not seem like sexy stuff, but to rise to C-level positions within any organization requires firsthand knowledge.

Third, always strive for a balance between *saying* and *doing* in matters related to your company's business. Wherever appropriate,

---

* A word of caution: *Knowing* what others' positions entail does not mean *telling* them how to do so, unless they actually ask for help or unless you're in a training situation. Being a know-it-all is usually the opposite of being a real leader.

make positive observations and suggestions, up, down, and across the organization. If your suggestions are not followed, never take it personally. Instead, look for every opportunity to volunteer for tasks and additional responsibilities. Interdisciplinary task forces and internal joint ventures are good places to start, especially if they jibe with your own growth cycle. You may find that your aspirations are different from those of the company, or you may find that they are aligned. In either case, you will have discovered a leapfrog moment.

Above all, pay attention and ask questions. Be curious about company plans and their expected benefits or outcomes, even if they don't affect you personally. Know where your organization stands in the competitive marketplace, who your customers are, and what their "customer journey" is really like. That knowledge, in addition to revealing potential career opportunities, is fertile ground for discovering your next leapfrog moment.

The true value of leapfrog moments, no matter when they happen or with whom you interact, is that they move *everyone* forward, especially if they are hungry for change. Even if you have to start over at some point (the subject of Chapter 3), you can do so with a new and often better point of view. So long as your dealings are honest and fair, the earned knowledge and contacts gained with each successive cycle cannot be taken away. In theory, it's possible to advance your position without this dynamic, at the expense of others, but in my experience it's not the kind of life you really want to have.

Always be prepared for the unexpected opportunity to leapfrog. Like battlefield promotions during war, leapfrog opportunities can be borne of unforeseen crises. When such openings present themselves, always be ready to jump into the breach, as it were.

At the end of the day, a leapfrog moment can move you more rapidly through the growth cycle you are currently in, or it can bypass some steps altogether, taking you directly to the next cycle and its GO moment. All it takes is your willingness to see the current status quo for what it is, a pattern of routine convenience that may or may not be helping you make real progress. If you're willing to take the risk (and the criticism), a leapfrog moment may be just the thing you need to move yourself forward.

Two Leapfrog Examples

Recently, my company sold two of its divisions to a private equity firm, a move that benefitted everyone involved. At the time the process began, both divisions were led by exceptional women in the prime of their careers. Both were offered the position of divisional president by the new owner over their respective divisions. One, Ann Hailer, stayed with the new company, while the other, Soo Jin Oh, left to pursue another opportunity. But both of them experienced profound leapfrog moments.

Of course I lobbied for both of them to stay with the buyer. To me, being the president of a private equity–owned company was a valuable career badge of honor—one that is hard to come by. After an objective appraisal of her new opportunity, Ann decided to accept the leadership position with the new company. Soo Jin on the other hand decided to leave, leveraging her time running a growth business for us into a new opportunity, as corporate chief of strategy for a large division at one of the largest media companies on the planet.

Both leaders' objective assessments of their respective career paths differed in specifics, but both experienced leapfrog moments. Each one found a way to disrupt their own status quo and begin a new growth cycle.

Exercise for the Reader

It's only natural to accept your current situation without question, even when (unknown to you) that situation is keeping you from moving forward. As you think about the stories and ideas in this chapter, try to recall an instance where the comfortable, normal status quo was upended, forcing you to look at your situation objectively.

Write down as much of the event as you can remember. As you do, answer these questions:

1. What precipitated the event? Did it arise from something you read or witnessed, or did someone bring something to your attention?
2. If it was the latter, was it a discussion that made you uncomfortable? (Bonus points for seeing past your discomfort.)
3. What was the "one thing"—an unexpected change of direction or purpose—that this event made clear in your mind?
4. Did you actually follow that leapfrog moment, and what were the results?

Chapter 3

Learning from Failure

> Next time, things won't be the same
> I'll make better choices and take the blame
> For all my actions and everything
> This is what life is
> —**Stefan Pruett (The Guidance), "Next Time"**

Abraham Lincoln is considered one of America's greatest presidents, but that was anything but obvious if you look at his early life. In his twenties, he failed in business (twice), lost an election, suffered through the death of a sweetheart, and had a nervous breakdown. In his thirties and forties he lost three more elections and failed in an effort to become vice president. Despite all this, as many historians have noted, Lincoln viewed defeat as a detour, not as a dead end.

Failure, in other words, is not only an unpleasant fact of life. It is also a means of achieving the things we want—if only we view it as such. In Silicon Valley, they say, "If you want to succeed, double your failure rate."

In the previous chapter, we focused on the *positive* moments that propel us from one phase of a growth cycle to another. Those leap-frog moments can be disguised as criticism or other unpleasantness, but, if we have sufficient objectivity and a thick skin, they are not intrinsically bad or traumatic experiences. Discovering a new path forward, or an entirely new growth cycle, is exhilarating, fulfilling, and well worth the bother of a few harsh words.

The same cannot be said of actual failure. When our best-laid plans fall apart, there are actual consequences, to our financial well-being, our relationships, and even our health. Failure is not just a feeling of embarrassment or regret, although those are often the byproducts. Failure is real; it causes pain and loss. So why is it a necessary facet of the GAIN model for growth?

On the Amazon subsidiary Goodreads.com, there are 125 books listed on the subject of failure. Specifically, they are all about how we can learn from failure—a much better teacher than success. In his most recent book, *The Power of Regret*, Daniel Pink declares that a "no regrets" philosophy of life is nonsensical, even dangerous. Regret, the natural byproduct of personal or professional failure, is actually something with the power to make us better. According to Pink, regret can improve our decisions, boost our performance, and deepen the meaning of actions (ours and others') that had a real, negative result.

While it may be possible to always succeed sequentially and it seems that some do, it is unlikely we're seeing or counting the failures at different stages of their development. "Success has many fathers, but failure is an orphan," as the saying goes. Once someone has a string of successes, they become pretty good at learning from failure and moving on. Therefore, that person is not calling a lot of attention to it. My failures are generally marked by the times in my career I resorted to consulting in between major projects.

So, if failure has such well-documented learning benefits, then why do we so often fail to learn from failure? How can we leverage failure to our advantage, speeding the steps in our current growth cycle or moving us more quickly to the next one?

The Anatomy of Failure and Loss

Failure is a complex subject. Inherently, our life is filled with failures from the very beginning. The only way we learn some of the most rudimentary skills is by trial and error: walking, talking, reading, riding a bike, or playing sports. When a child skins a knee, flubs a word, or drops a ball, they are a step closer to doing things differently and, with the right response from others (and themselves), mastering the skill to a greater or lesser degree. Even with more advanced skills and knowledge, we all struggle and fail in the beginning.

Most of us think of failure as having something (at least in our minds) and then losing it, especially when it comes to possessions, athletic contests, or business. When it comes to work and business, losing is often defined as being stuck in a dead-end job, getting fired, or having success and then losing the source or position. (It goes without saying that these failures often result in the loss of income or possessions.)

But because winning is so ingrained in our competitive culture, it's hard to accept the fact that failure is a normal part of everything we do. Every aspect of life includes elements of failure, whether they be economic, social, physical, psychological, or relational. Often it's a combination of all or some of the above. It can be large or small, broad or narrow in its consequences for others. It can involve a rejection or negation of your ideas, your actions, or your personality. So why is it an important concept—one that deserves much closer attention? And why do we so often view failure as something to be avoided at any cost?

Most people agree that failure is a motivator—or at least it can be. It positions you to feel and act differently than you did before it occurred. The trick of course is to manage that motivation in such a way that your subsequent actions benefit yourself and others, rather than becoming an impediment to such actions. In my experience, that is easier said than done. Failure in our culture carries strong emotions, which can lead to responses that Daniel Kahneman* and others refer to as "System 1," a part of our makeup that "operates automatically and quickly, with little or no effort and no sense of voluntary control." This is often at odds with the other, "System 2" aspect of our nature, one that "allocates attention to the effortful mental activities that demand it, including complex calculations." Thus, the strong emotions attached to failure, while they may have a positive result in simpler situations, like riding a bike, can work against you in a complex one.

So, to help frame the issue better, and develop better responses to failure, let's take a look at the three components of failure itself:

Failure is always related to a plan of some kind. This is when things go badly, either there was no plan, a flawed plan, or the plan was just not followed, deliberately or otherwise. Usually it's a combination. You would think that calmly examining the plan or its absence, and

---

* Kahneman's insightful, five-hundred-page book, *Thinking, Fast and Slow*, discusses these aspects of normal human nature in great detail, including the fact that we often take the path of least resistance, which leads us to make cognitive errors out of unconscious bias.

the steps taken (or not) would be the rational response to any failure. Unfortunately, this is frequently undermined by the fact that . . .

Failure and responsibility are not always connected. One of our favorite national pastimes is blaming someone (possibly ourselves) when things go badly or wrong. But the sobering fact is that failure is *not* always caused by someone acting (or not acting) according to plan. Sometimes it's totally outside anyone's control. But whether or not there is a responsible party, the third factor is that . . .

Failure always produces a strong emotional response. Take your pick. The emotions following a moment of failure range from disappointment and disgust to fear and anger, depending on the seriousness of the consequences. There's no question that these emotions are negative and unpleasant—so much so that they stay with you long after the event itself is over. In fact, studies have shown that in our long-term memory, negative information is better remembered than neutral or positive information.

Think about that for a moment. You can likely remember when the planes hit the World Trade Center in 2001, but can you remember what movie won the Oscar for Best Picture? The same thing happens, to a lesser degree (thankfully) when we experience any sort of failure. It's a natural, evolutionary response. Our ancestors (the uneaten ones) developed keen, detailed memories of their mishaps and close encounters with danger. Those memories in turn helped them develop strategies—plans to ensure their survival.

Today, when we experience failure, no matter the cause, the strong accompanying emotions can either hinder or help us. They can discourage us from further action, cause us to retreat, or spur us to hunt for scapegoats. But they are also potential allies in pursuing a growth cycle. By making our memories more indelible, failure may become a powerful instructor.

Failure is seldom a single, well-defined event, isolated from other professional and personal circumstances. Very often, failure happens unexpectedly, when there are other problems to manage. But the results, however unwelcome, can be surprising.

About thirty years ago, after a successful career in media, finance, and deal making, I closed my practice to pursue a different life. I became the owner of a business I knew absolutely nothing about. In retrospect, I now realize I embarked on the NEXT phase of my previous cycle, and the GO phase of this one, without having implemented the ASSESS and IDENTIFY phases of either one.

What I chose to pursue was the wholesale and retail, new and used auto parts business. At the time, I blithely assumed that I could just apply modern marketing and sales techniques to a creaky old business—much as I had done with radio and television stations. What I did was like putting a supercharger on a weak four-cylinder engine without upgrading the other parts needed to withstand the added torque. In other words, I failed to understand the mechanics of the business model.

During my brief tenure, I increased sales dramatically, but the changing nature of the business resulted in spiking costs for handling and inventory. The competition had also shifted. DIY chains like AutoZone were expanding. Later-model, more computerized cars required a larger, more complex parts inventory. What the previous owners knew (and I failed to understand) was that traditional parts stores were increasingly unable to compete with high-profit, low-workload DIY chains.

Faced with some very pissed off and frankly vindictive creditors, my only recourse was to file for personal bankruptcy. I was completely broke. Intellectually, I knew the cause of the failure, and had learned a very valuable, albeit expensive lesson in retail economics. But the emotional toll was a different matter. Although my wife was fortunately protected from financial loss, we both experienced the shock and lasting trauma of failure.

Not long afterward, I returned to deal-making mode in the media world. I took on major roles in various private, public, and PE-owned companies. Having learned from my failed venture, my financial recovery was remarkable. To outward appearances, I had fixed the problem and was on my next GO phase. However, internally and secretly, I still carried the burden of financial failure. I was hanging on to the negative, emotional repercussions, unable to let go and fully apply myself to the next growth cycle in my career. Even though I went on to be tremendously successful, I feel that hanging on to these old wounds limited my true potential.

All that changed when I faced a moment of failure I could not fix. In 2007, I was still carrying the emotional burden of my now-distant financial failure in auto parts. But that year, my youngest son passed away at age twenty. All our plans as a family were upended permanently; we had no control whatsoever. In the midst of the shock and grief and turmoil, I had a startling revelation. Death is unfixable—the ultimate school of hard lessons. In that traumatic moment, the burden of my previous failure took on a different meaning. It made me aware of the facts in a new light.

The truth was, every other thing in my life either did not matter or could be fixed. Carrying around the emotional "rock" of a fixable failure (or picking it up in the first place) was no longer an option I cared about. We all pick up emotional "rocks," which we carry around and allow to weigh us down and prevent us from living life to the fullest. Some, like the loss of a child or loved one, you never put down, but sometimes you can rest them on a mental shelf and give yourself a break. One thing you never should do is pick up the emotional rocks of others, whether it is your spouse's family, people at work, or political beliefs and causes. Do not carry other people's rocks. It is critical you make important decisions and take up the things that give you energy rather than weigh yourself down with other people's problems. The same holds true for holding on to business or personal failures. That's not to say you shouldn't own your responsibility, but you can't keep carrying mistakes like a bag of rocks.

I wish I could say that was the end of the lesson. Our family pulled it together and supported each other through it all. But in 2020, my oldest son also passed away due to congestive heart failure stemming from a congenital heart defect. My family perseveres to this day, but the lessons of extreme loss and its trauma are ongoing.

At a bare minimum, such events put all failures and triumphs into perspective. A business failure can seem like a death—of your cherished plans and goals, that is. It can even derail your current growth cycle, or at least delay it. But when the truly important things, particularly family, are taken away, all else becomes more complicated. The loss of a loved one is a completely different category and a very individual process. Somehow, some way, you learn to absorb it and live with it. There is no way to live without it, and at times it will stop you in your tracks. It doesn't get better; it just becomes a part of you that you learn to deal with.

Since then, I have certainly backslid from time to time, picking up and carrying the emotional rock of a business failure—or even the lesser burden of the lack of greater achievement. But for the most part, those losses have taught me to treat failure in context, accept the emotional response for what it's worth, clean up the mess, and move forward. Never waste time beating yourself up over a failure or comparing yourself with someone else who is more successful than you. No matter how rich or successful you are, there will always be someone you think has it better. No matter how successful you become, you will always have things you see as failures.

The emotional experience following any failure can easily limit growth by making us more timid and risk averse. If we bottle it up and hope the feeling goes away, we are less likely to learn from it and add to our ASSESS and IDENTIFY phases of growth. But if we allow it to clarify the facts, examine the plan, and hold people justly responsible, it can make real growth happen more often.

The Art of Failing Faster

Another helpful way to look at this issue is the notion of *failing faster*. This is a prevalent approach in software development and is of course a key aspect of science itself. More recently, the notion has become popular within the general business community, but with some misconceptions attached.

Failing faster does not mean allowing business failures to accumulate or taking a fatalistic attitude toward them. Rather it means taking proactive steps to learn from them and adjust the plan accordingly. It also means owning one's individual responsibility for clearly defined pieces of the plan. Most importantly, failing faster requires subjecting the plan to *testing*—putting it through a real-world situation where the results can easily be measured. The more cycles deliberately applied and examined, the greater the likelihood of a positive outcome. Learning from each measured result, failed or successful, can be key to assessing and identifying the best way forward.

The notion of failing faster can be tricky. It means you must determine when to give up on a *project*, which is far different from giving up on a *dream*. Failing faster today is often referred to as pivoting, which is basically repurposing your business plan to find a path to profitability within existing resources. Perhaps this comes out of something you discovered in your product or service mix that wasn't your main goal. Pivots can be applicable to the entire project or just certain segments of it. Often, pivots involve some downsizing or less additional investment. The theory is to get to a profit and then figure it out from there.

Failing faster, successfully, is based on decisions you must make in the moment. You are the main determinant of defining your failure point. Usually this decision is about time and money, and on refocusing energy on areas where you can sustain efforts with income or capital. This is in contrast with absolute financial failure, where you run out of money, the ability to produce income, and ultimately the means to continue the endeavor in any form. That does not have to be the case; ideally, you may have options to create an orderly shutdown and start again, in a more difficult version of the NEXT phase. This might include preserving some of your capital, selling assets, or helping place people you have worked with in order to preserve relationships. But as I can attest, it's not always possible to absorb failure neatly.

Other types of failures that fall outside the "fail faster" model include losing your job, losing a relationship, or just making poor decisions as a participant in society. These usually offer no recourse, no "do-over" opportunities, to salvage a lost situation. But they can provide the basis for making different decisions in subsequent cycles. In that way, failure can be the basis for the ASSESS process, helping you measure where you are in the cycle and what needs to be adjusted—in terms of behavior, capital, or other resources—in order to move forward.

Failing faster is easier to do in a scientific context, where experimentation is the norm, than it is in business generally. Where performance and profitability are rigidly connected, it is difficult if not impossible to plan an experiment whose failure may have disastrous consequences.

The answer is not to put everyone under a microscope and analyze their failures. In theory, this may produce actionable results, but the toll it takes on morale is in itself a failure with predictably poor outcomes. Instead, a better approach to failing faster is an application of the growth cycle model—more specifically, the use of *mini*-growth cycles.

Today, in my own ventures within our company, I am still guided by the idea of developing ideas quickly and leveraging sub-optimized assets in order to limit risk until we can get a workable proof of concept. It is preferable to agonizing in committees and worrying about failure when starting something that needs to launch on a companywide scale. First prove it on the street, on a smaller scale. See how it goes. You can always accelerate once you have more data.

Applying mini–growth cycles requires that a company be open to but not governed by a "what if" culture. Above all, it must never stigmatize failure. When a team member fails in a particular task, large or small, and in the process unearths a barrier to NEXT, it should be cause for celebration.

Failure and Growth Cycles

With a better understanding of failure itself, and how it involves a plan (or a lack of one), degrees of responsibility and control, and especially an emotional impact, let's examine each of the phases of a growth cycle and see how failure can make them more effective.

At the GO stage, it is especially important not to let the trauma of a past failure deter you from pursuing that "one thing" with every part of your being. If the past is particularly fraught, this may mean confiding in a qualified coach or mentor.

One of the benefits of the GO phase is that it is inherently optimistic. Even in the face of conventional wisdom or peer pressure, the urge to act on inspiration is a powerful one. It is certainly a powerful archetype in most cultures, especially in the hero myths we all admire. Audacity and overcoming adversity, even if that adversity is largely emotional, are deeply ingrained in most of us.

Failure, handled well, is an excellent tutor at the start of any growth cycle. While early cycles may start with a degree of naivete (as mine certainly did), later ones are usually better informed by past failures.

At the ASSESS stage, failure can be the fuel that propels you forward. This is not only the "lessons learned" in a failed situation but also the emotion accompanying failure. The natural shock experienced when things go wrong makes the facts and circumstances clearer and remembered longer. Just as death or tragedy puts everything else in context, so also can the memory of failure clarify even seemingly trivial details.

This is not automatic or guaranteed, however. When blame becomes the primary response, then emotional trauma can also create a distorted view of things. This is when the ASSESS phase requires a double helping of facts *not* related to the failure. It's also a good reason to let the ASSESS phase run its course. Failure is almost always more complicated than we feel it is, with *some* people or groups responsible for *parts* of it, and some aspects beyond anyone's control. Finding that balanced response is one reason why this stage should take two or three years.

At the IDENTIFY stage, past failure is one of your best allies. During this period, counterfeit notions can emerge, each one posing as the mindset shift you've been hoping for. But with an informed knowledge of part failures, including your own, your chances of detecting these counterfeits increase.

This does not guarantee success, but it does improve your chances. Whether your moment of identification is about your career, your business, or both, a healthy respect for failure will get you to your pivotal moment with fewer detours and distractions.

Finally, **at the NEXT stage**, experience with failure will help you avoid the pitfalls while simultaneously preparing for the future *and* making sure you're not leaving a mess when you go. As we discussed earlier, acting impulsively on your new vision can cause more harm than good, especially when you hold a position of power and responsibility.

During this phase, you need to be adept at *avoiding* failure. That means seeing beyond your own personal ASSESS and IDENTIFY process and perceiving the growth cycles of those around you—and of the company as a whole. At the executive level, this is especially important. A blind leap into one's personal "next big thing" often spells disaster in a large or publicly traded company. Even at lower, managerial levels, the NEXT phase must be treated with awareness and diplomacy.

As we've seen, failure is not an end in itself, nor is it the death of one's hopes and aspirations. It can be traumatic or merely uncomfortable, but it always has the potential to move you more effectively through your present growth cycle and on to the next one.

Exercise for the Reader

Failure is always uncomfortable, often embarrassing, and frequently with results that must be undone or compensated for. Despite all this, try to recount a significant instance of failure in your business or personal life. Ask yourself the following questions:

1. Was the failure due to your actions, the actions of others, of both you and others, or neither one? A failure that occurred outside your control can be just as traumatic as one you helped create—and just as likely to contain the seeds of change.
2. What was your initial emotion related to the event? Did the failure create a memory you find it hard (or impossible) to forget?

3. What was your instinctive first response to that emotion? Were you tempted to withdraw or just toss in your hand, so to speak? (There's no wrong answer here. We're human.)
4. What new knowledge or insights did this failure reveal? Did you act on them, and what were the results?

Chapter 4

The Importance of Resilience and Persistence

> Everything's out there, we're climbing up these walls
> Falling down the stairs laced with sweat and tears
> It's time to pick ourselves back up
> Show the world we're tough, I may never know
> Because something is out there waiting for you to find it
> And when you do, it may hit you oh so blindly
> Pick ourselves back up, show the world we're tough
> Stop running on an engine of fear!
> —**Stefan Pruett (Peachcake), "Don't Panic, It's Organic"**

Resilience is a theme in nearly every epic tale, from the book of Job to *Deadpool*. We root for the underdog, feel every blow, celebrate every comeback win, and hope that same resilience resides in us.

It does. Depending on the "shape" you were in before facing any of life's challenges, you are genetically predisposed to spring back to your original form, or to something even more suitable to your chosen course of action. It takes a lot of wearing down and social pressure to undo what eons of evolution have built into our instinct to adapt and bounce back.

As an element of growth cycles, resilience is important on many levels, from our evolution as a species (actually, all species) to our response to the events, good and bad, in our personal and professional lives.

The word *resilience* has two meanings. Literally, it means elasticity or "the ability of a substance or object to spring back into shape" after bending, stretching, or being compressed. That should immediately bring the metaphorical meaning to mind. Resiliency denotes toughness, in a person or an animal. It is "the capacity to withstand or recover quickly from difficulties."

A Choice, Not a Guarantee

Speaking of evolution, it's important to remember that, while resilience is a characteristic of every living species, and of life in general, it is not a guaranteed outcome for every individual. We see resilience in nature, sometimes against long odds, but as every nature documentary proves, not every living creature survives. What distinguishes us from the doomed gazelle, I believe, is our greater ability to reason and choose our path.

Unfortunately, in these times, it's entirely possible for human beings to lose this ability—to give up in the face of adversity. When

I see a person *not* exhibiting resiliency, I imagine it's like a ball of tinfoil being crushed into smaller and smaller dimensions until it's a fraction of its original shape and size. I have seen people exhibit these tendencies, psychologically, which is a scary thought, as I've felt these tendencies in my own journey. In the face of adversity and uncertainty (since we're *not* in a movie), it is tempting to say, "enough is enough," meaning "I am done," as opposed to, "I am going to return to who I really am or become who I want to be."

Both of these responses are mental states, based wholly on personal belief, to be followed up by actions. Our resilience is not guaranteed, but we can make choices even in difficult times. Deep down, I believe that no one wants to become like a crushed ball of tinfoil. We'd much rather spring back to our original shape, or to an even better one. We have the built-in capacity to recover lost resiliency, and to develop and refine it, like any other physical or mental ability.

Resilience is the glue that makes growth cycles, leapfrog moments, and positive responses to failure all come together. It is a key component of thriving in the midst of apparent difficulty. It is also a component of every aspect of a growth cycle, as we will see in a bit, but it is especially relevant during the NEXT phase.

Resilience involves creating a positive response to being knocked off balance and deterred from moving forward. This comes in many forms, one of the most common occurring when we run into *rejection*. This can be a rejection of an idea you hold dear. It can also be a rejection of you personally. Sometimes, it's both. It takes an extra dose of confidence and persistence to rebound from this level of rejection, since it affects you at your core. Persistence is the ability to keep going when things appear to be adverse to the desired outcome.

In the paragraphs that follow, I tell how my experience in learning persistence and resilience formed my approach to rejection for the rest of my career. I hesitated to include it because the example is from decades ago. Since then, local media platforms have evolved, and frankly newspapers themselves have evolved into digital media platforms. While today Google, Facebook, and Instagram are large local platforms, the point of the story and response to rejection remains just as fresh and relevant as ever. Just substitute modern platforms, challenges, and modern dialogue. When rejected, gather more intelligence and keep going back with good ideas or potential.

At age twenty-one, I first started to learn resilience, and overcoming rejection, as an ad salesperson for KPLR television in St. Louis. In general, advertising is not the ideal career for those who can't handle rejection, but in the 1970s, local TV advertising was particularly tough. At the time, national brands were spending big bucks on TV, but the dominant advertising medium for *local* businesses was newspapers.* Business owners and their ad buyers (if they even had them) had limited budgets and an automatic "no" to new salespeople with unfamiliar products. They were always insanely busy and were usually comfortable with their existing advertising products—and with the salesmen they had known for years.

Knowing it would be an uphill climb, I developed a deep knowledge of newspaper advertising, how it worked, what it cost, and the kind of results advertisers could expect. (For those of you keeping

---

* This was *way* before digital and mobile came along and turned advertising on its head.

score, this was a big part of my ASSESS phase.) I developed a sales pitch that showed advertisers how they could reduce their newspaper cost by 50 percent over time and multiply their market reach by adding local TV advertising. The math was solid. By switching from a weekly "double truck" newspaper ad* to a single page, their visibility and readership was reduced by only 25 percent, but it cut their cost in half. With that savings, they could buy a TV ad for four times a day for an entire month! It was a surefire formula that just couldn't miss. That is, until I met Gil Varn, the head of Varn Aluminum Siding.

Every Saturday evening, I would get my hands on the first edition of the massive Sunday *St. Louis Post-Dispatch*. I pored over each issue, looking for the full-color "double truck" ads. This was where the big money was. These were placed by businesses fully committed to big newspaper ad budgets but who rarely used TV. I knew I could show them I could increase the efficiency of their ad spend. It was brilliant! And one Sunday I found the perfect candidate: Varn Aluminum Siding.

The next day, I pulled into the Varn parking lot in my rusty, beat-up MGB. The lot looked like part of a converted gas station, but it was filled with new Cadillacs and Lincolns, like a scene from the movie *Tin Men*. I went inside where I saw a very large man sitting behind a tiny desk. When I asked to see the owner, the large man promptly told me that the owner was Gil Varn, and that he wasn't in. I left my card and said, "I'll be back." Undaunted, I continued to show up, in the same beat-up MGB next to all those fancy cars, and got the same answer from the large man behind the tiny desk,

---

* For those who don't speak ancient newspaper jargon, that's a full-color, two-page centerspread ad. And yes, it cost advertisers a bundle.

until something eventually dawned on me. As you probably guessed, the large man was in fact the mysterious Mr. Gil Varn. I was being rejected out of hand, with zero chance to explain my idea. I was getting pretty thick-skinned by then, so emotionally I was OK, but I was stumped.

In this case, resilience came as a combination of luck and a strategic "mindset shift" on my part. Late one afternoon, I picked up a call from a media buyer from Little Rock, Arkansas. She wanted to place an ad schedule for an aluminum siding company for $8,000 a week. That happened to be the equivalent of a full-color double truck newspaper ad, so you can probably guess where this is going.

I took the order for the Little Rock advertiser, jumped into my MGB, and sped over to Varn Aluminum Siding. When the big man at the tiny desk told me that Mr. Varn was not in, I "left him a message," namely that a new competitor had just come in with a massive TV ad schedule. I left the building, but the next morning I had a message from the big man at the tiny desk—Mr. Gil Varn. He wanted to buy a TV schedule matching that of his competitor. He wanted my station to handle everything, including producing the spot. I did finally get a chance to prove my point, but that week I went from being the no-account newbie sales guy to being one of the largest local billers on the station. Those two accounts changed my entire game, in unexpected and fortuitous ways. For me, it was an object lesson that resilience plus persistence (and knowledge) always prevails.

Resilience in this case had a lot to do with the IDENTIFY phase of that particular cycle, plus my willingness to seize the opportunity with both hands. My commission that month was $6,000, the equivalent of $60,000 in 2023 dollars.

Take the definition of resilience, "to recover quickly from difficulties," at face value. It is a constant, not only in one's career growth but also in life itself. Everything we learn to do, from crawling, walking, and beyond, involves difficulties from which we naturally recover. Much of today's culture, including modern parenting, has focused on processes that humans used to take for granted. It dwells on the difficulty of every aspect of our development and obsesses about everything that can go wrong. Fortunately, 99 percent of human beings overcome these challenges and manage to become functional, mobile, and able to communicate.

We have to conclude that resiliency is part of our DNA; it defines our humanity. To be sure, our society creates new obstacles all the time, tempting us to crumple instead of spring back. But that is all the more reason to *decide* to be resilient. We must consciously decide to GO when the opportunity arises. We must look into the how and why of things, to ASSESS our path by investigation, research, and interaction. We must make the mental judgments and calculations necessary to IDENTIFY that mindset shift we've been seeking. And above all, we must determine our NEXT course of action, and have the courage and wisdom to pursue it.

The Psychology of Resilience and Persistence Go Hand in Hand

In general, the word *resilient* is used in psychology to describe people who, despite suffering stressful situations, manage to overcome them and not be psychologically hobbled by them. The Resilience Project, a European research initiative, defines it as "the ability to succeed in a way that is acceptable to society despite stress or adversity that usually entails a serious risk of negative outcomes" and "a process of competitiveness where the person must adapt positively to adverse situations (resilienceproject.eu/the-history-of-resilience)." They also describe it as a "maintenance of skills despite continuous stress," which fits perfectly in the context of growth cycles.

Some people are naturally resilient, with personalities that make it easier to "keep your head when all about you are losing theirs and blaming it on you." Such people are usually good communicators and are good at managing their emotions and making realistic plans. They also tend to view themselves as fighters, not victims of circumstances. But these traits are not limited to the chosen few. Far from it. Resilience is something everyone can build in themselves and even nurture in others.

There are proven ways to develop greater resilience in yourself, even if you're not born with it. One is to *reframe negative thoughts* that accompany every setback or obstacle, large or small. Our brains are hardwired to focus on the negative since that's how our ancestors managed to survive and eventually produce us! The problem is that the stress-producing stuff is ubiquitous these days. It's in our daily diet of news, work, and personal interactions. Then the setbacks and obstacles pile on and slam us with negative thoughts that trigger our fight-or-flight reflex. But if we make a habit of reframing—looking for small ways to tackle a problem and make changes that will help the situation—we can become more resilient over time.

This habit works well if you do something that seems obvious but gets lost in the moment: *focus on the things you can control.* No matter how dire a situation may be, there's always something constructive to do—something that has a measurable result, even if it only incrementally helps with the situation. (In my experience, a series of these "incremental" actions quite often moves the bigger problem further than you imagined.) Resilience often flows from having a plan of the things you can actually *do*, from choosing where to put your attention and what to leave alone.

Another way to develop greater resilience tends to be overlooked in today's competitive environment: *seek support*. Later in the book, we'll discuss the kinds of people and situations that will help you optimize growth cycles. But for now, just realize that personal resilience seldom thrives in a vacuum. Sharing concerns with a trusted ally not only reinforces protective factors like executive function and emotional maturity, but it also may shed light on the actual problem you're facing and give you answers you hadn't considered. Imagine that!

Finally, one of the most important ways to build resilience is quite simple: *remember that suffering and stress do not discriminate*. There is no world out there where people experience only success and never suffer setbacks, obstacles, or outright disasters. You are not the target of some plot to exclude you from that world. Your problems are common to every other human, as are the solutions. Knowing that will put things in perspective, and help you take them on.

How Resilience and Persistence Fuel the GAIN Cycle

Resilience is bouncing back, returning to your former shape, or a better one. Persistence is the ability to keep going in the face of what happened in rejection or loss. So, if resilience is the glue that holds the steps of a growth cycle together, then we need to take a closer look at each phase with that habit in mind.

In ***the GO phase***, resilience is usually more prevalent when you've already experienced multiple cycles. Think about it. It's easier to start something if you don't know much about life. But later on, experiences in your business or personal life are never completely free from trauma, so starting out the next time may require more resilience on your part. When I was a headstrong kid, I had zero trouble chasing after Grandmother when I knew she was the "one thing" I wanted. But after a few hard knocks, the decision to GO for something required an internal pep talk or two.

For me, the start of a growth cycle always benefitted from my past experiences of reframing negative thoughts, focusing on the things I could control, and seeking the support of trusted allies. The more experience I had in the practice of resilience, the more confident I became at the start of each new adventure.

In the ASSESS and IDENTIFY phases, think of resilience as a keel of sorts, helping you balance the pressure of ideas and information (the sails in this metaphor) with a sense of reality and perspective. There is so much information available for you to assess and quantify; having practical experience with challenges and measured responses will keep the panic to a minimum. Personal resilience will increase confidence—your sense of "I've been there before" and "I've got this," which will help filter out distractions that can seem alarming. Having dealt calmly with problems in the past will help you frame potential problems that arise during the ASSESS stage.

This is important as you approach the mindset shift part of the journey. With each successive cycle, being calm and resilient will help you identify the real moment when it happens and filter out the counterfeits that arise.

Finally, ***in the NEXT phase***, resilience is absolutely essential in keeping everything else on track while you simultaneously plan your move to the pending GO phase. The higher you are in an organization, the greater the pressures and potential for chaos. No matter how well you explain your own trajectory, and take steps to make others whole, there are sure to be moments of chaos and disruption—misunderstandings that could threaten not only your NEXT phase, but also your reputation and effectiveness as a leader.

Like every other stressful situation, the "bumps" of the last stage of a growth cycle can be handled either well or poorly. Being resilient in these situations should be thought of as a master class of sorts. Departing from one executive position to take on an entirely new direction creates opportunities to reframe negative thoughts (every day, in my experience), stay focused on things you *can* control, and remember to keep everything in its proper context.

Conclusions and Next Steps

As your position in any organization rises, it will entail more responsibilities, and an ever greater likelihood of barriers and setbacks. As those increase, so will the need for personal and professional resilience. When working on any growth cycle, persistence and resilience are not "nice-to-have" options. They are *essential requirements* to making that cycle meaningful, manageable, and impactful.

Before moving on to Part Two, think about the basics of growth cycles, from the GO moment through ASSESS, IDENTIFY, and NEXT. Spend some time with your exercise responses at the end of each chapter thus far, and feel free to add to them. You will find, as we talk about implementing these cycles in your own situation, that the examples will help you establish new habits that can last a lifetime.

Exercise for the Reader

In this exercise, write down what you can recall about how you "bounced back" from an adverse or traumatic experience in your life. If you wrote about a notable failure in the previous chapter's exercise, you can use that as your example of resilience. Or you can select any other noteworthy event. As you recount the events and your responses, answer these questions:

What was your original or baseline "shape" (your financial or career situation, your emotional state, or anything else you think is relevant) *before* you experienced the adverse event or circumstance?

How did that "shape" change under the pressure of the event? Did you have any biases or preconceived notions that made the event seem unexpected or even shocking?

During the adverse event, to what extent did you focus on things *within* your control? To what extent did you dwell on things *outside* your control?

How often did you ask the question, "Is what I'm doing helping or harming me?"

To what extent did you return to (or even exceed) your original state following the event?

Did the event (and your recovery) inform the way you assess your current situation and identify new potential? List at least three things that changed as a result.

PART TWO

APPLYING GROWTH CYCLES

Chapter 5

Growth Cycles in Action

When in doubt, do something.
—**Steve Pruett**

Over two centuries ago, a group of weary soldiers was busily at work, digging what was to be a defensive fortification in a conflict that had been dragging on for years without much success. Their commanding officer was issuing orders when a man in civilian clothes approached, asking why the officer was not helping the men dig. Not impressed with the "I'm in charge" answer, the man dismounted and helped the men finish the task. Before leaving, he had words of praise for the men and some astute observations for the officer, who only then recognized him as General George Washington.

I began writing this book because I wanted to encourage others as they develop extraordinary, successful careers for themselves. In short, I want them to become better leaders, since being a leader is a critical factor when it comes to optimizing the GAIN model. Of course, "leader" means different things to different people. Like me, you may be on the entrepreneur track, always seeking the next new or disruptive thing, tackling big challenges as you lead your business or nonprofit. Or you may consider yourself more of a key contributor, a rising star player on a dynamic business team. Or you may be a "behind the scenes" facilitator, shunning the spotlight but always looking to fill in the gaps and increase the velocity of your business or nonprofit.

No matter which one of these leadership types you are, you always need to grow, and to expand your capacity for success. You need to address the needs of multiple stakeholders and team members—including yourself! As a leader, you have to conceive and execute strategies, by yourself and with others, take advantage of leapfrog moments, and practice resilience and persistence in the face of failure. To do this, it's essential to consciously apply the steps of GAIN laid out in Part One.

The fact that you are reading this book tells me that you are already in a GO phase of your career, whether or not you recognize it as such, and however early or late in that career you may be. Even if the driver of that decision is unclear or seems coincidental, the fact is you've made a decision and have decided to make the best of it. That means it's time to do the ASSESS part, to find out *where* you are, *why* you're there, and *what* can make this stage of your career more effective. As we'll see, this will help you IDENTIFY the right inflection point—that "one thing" that will ultimately lead you to the NEXT phase of your life.

Different Careers, Same Principles

The principles laid out in Part 1 were derived from my years of experience, first in sales, then in investment banking, company ownership, and C-level executive roles at large public and private companies. I have also had a remarkable, somewhat unique family life that informed and inspired my thinking. In many ways, I've been blessed, but I know that you're in different, perhaps less fortunate circumstances. You have different life experiences, a different career path, and different ideas on what it means to succeed. So, we need to look at growth cycles from multiple points of view to see how they apply to situations like yours.

In hindsight, I now realize that my "superpower" was in recognizing and seizing leapfrog opportunities as they occurred. I just went with my instincts, going for the thing I really wanted to do, being happy doing it, and being as good at it as I could possibly be. I know that involved a high degree of nerve on my part. But I also know that I could have done better—and avoided more missteps—if I had asked more questions, examined my assumptions more deliberately, and sought out more resources earlier in the process. I could have been more purposeful!

Asking the Questions

In this chapter, I'll walk you through some hypothetical career trajectories, pointing out different points of opportunity and choice that can supercharge your growth cycles and increase your advantage.

When I faced my own inflection points, my mind was flooded with questions. So each example will come with questions that our hypothetical person should be asking, the likely answers, and some of the reasons why those answers matter.

You might say, "That's fine for a hypothetical example, but what if my answers are different?" For example, in my experience, the ASSESS question, "Am I in a position or role that excites me?" is often answered with a positive. But if the answer for you is no, then my hypothetical scenario will make less sense. When I pose such an open-ended question in what follows, I'll mark it with an asterisk* and ask you to bear with me.

Looking back, I can reconstruct the important drivers at work in my own life, and the guardrails that kept me on course. Although our experiences differ, I trust that these hypotheticals and the questions that accompany them will help you see *your* inflection points and drivers for yourself.

Scenario #1: The Business of Making Things

For our first hypothetical career path, we'll look at the world of growing or building, assembling, packaging, and selling actual *things*. This covers a huge range of tangible products: spinach, smartphones, swimsuits, and solar panels. It can also include things we did not actually make, like real estate, but have found ways to improve upon and convince others to buy. In fact, there's a large area of overlap of intangible *services* like advertising and supply chain logistics with the world of making things for people to buy and use.

Our hypothetical example in this sector is a middle manager whom we'll call Soledad. Her company is a large printing operation, specializing in custom sign displays for retailers and trade show events, with a somewhat vague corporate mandate to expand into new markets and create new, large-scale promotional products. Soledad began her career as a production line worker and occasional designer, but she was soon promoted to a position overseeing the production of in-store signage products. She clearly had the skills and drive that brought her this far, but she knew there must be more she could do.

Through trial and error, someone like Soledad would very likely find a way to advance her career. But let's take a closer look at how the GAIN model could accelerate that process. Here are the steps:

> ## Identify the GO Moment
>
> What was your desired objective at the time? Is it still a valid goal?* When and how did it become clear in your mind? What were the aspects of that objective that made it desirable? What were the obstacles? What made you choose to go forward, despite those obstacles?

For nearly everyone in Soledad's position, they have already experienced that initial GO phase—seeing something they knew they wanted and deciding to go for it. The first part of leveraging growth cycles is not just to GO, but to understand why you did. In Soledad's case, she had seen the potential of what she was making (signs) and knew she could find more efficient ways of getting the job done. She certainly exhibited innovation, leadership, and drive. She also believed that there must be new and better products to complement or even surpass the existing ones.

Understanding your own reasons for moving forward is critical; you didn't get where you are by accident. By asking these *what, when,* and *why* questions, Soledad established a foundation for understanding her GO moment, which is the context for the next stage.

> ## Diligently ASSESS the Current Situation
>
> Are you in a position or role that excites you and engages your imagination?* Why does it excite you?* What would make it better or more exciting? What is the current state of your own skills? What are the skills of your colleagues? What is the current state of technology in your field? What are the technology trends that will affect your field in the near term? What do you need to manage your team and work with executives and partners more effectively?

The first question is key. If Soledad loves what she is doing, the rest of the ASSESS questions will follow easily. If not, then it's time to insert other questions, beginning with *why* it doesn't excite her, and whether she made the right GO decision. There are times when career decisions are made *for* you, out of desperate financial situations, for example. But even in those situations, a conscious assessment of the situation is still the right thing to do. Honing one's skills and knowledge will accelerate growth, either in the career path you love or in the one you're aiming for.

In the manufacturing sector, there is no shortage of expertise on ways to improve one's "hard skills"—ways to do the work more effectively. From equipment manufacturer support to trade associations and supplemental training programs, Soledad and her team can choose from an array of helpful resources. Similarly, the resources for learning "soft skills," such as continuous improvement and lean manufacturing programs, are readily available.

But practical, skill-building resources are only the beginning. For Soledad, books like Liz Wiseman's *Multipliers* and Daniel Pink's *Drive* were the building blocks for her suite of managerial skills—a suite that will serve her well in subsequent growth cycles. From Wiseman, she learned more about the distinctions between the "idea killer" manager, one who insists on putting their opinions and reputation first, and the "multiplier" leader, one who engages with the creativity of their members and consciously avoids being the center of attention. From Pink's book, she learned the distinction between *extrinsic* motivation (the carrot-and-stick approach) and *intrinsic* motivation, the innate desire for autonomy, mastery, and purpose. For her team, the idea of reading books may seem like homework, so motivational exercises and events may be a better source of information.

Books are of course only one resource for the ASSESS phase. As we'll explore in Chapter 8, there are many types of allies and influencers that can help accelerate the GAIN growth cycle process. A live coach or mentor with good qualifications is always at the top of the list, but in my experience books are the next best thing.

For Soledad, the ASSESS process began shortly after her promotion—her GO moment. For most people, this phase can last three or four years, although the habit of learning and gaining new information is a lifelong process. For Soledad, it took only two years of exploration to come upon the third phase of the cycle.

Recognize the IDENTIFY Moment

During the assessment process, did an event or trend stand out as a mindset shift for you and your role in your industry?

> Did it resonate with you personally?* Does it represent an unexpected, leapfrog moment in your career—even one that may start an entirely new growth cycle? To what extent is it based on known technology or industry practices? Is there an element of fantasy or wishful thinking involved? Does it resonate with you personally? Is it worth the time, effort, and risk involved?

This is the most exciting part of the GAIN model, and also the most prone to unconscious bias. As we'll explore in Chapter 6, human beings naturally see patterns where there are none. We tend to "go with our gut," seeing what we want to see instead of what's actually there. That does not mean an IDENTIFY moment cannot be outlandish or unexpected. It simply means that we have to look at it carefully, just as we did in the ASSESS phase. That means asking hard questions, like "Is it really feasible?" and following the answers, wherever they lead.

For Soledad, her moment was a logical outgrowth of her current work. Signage printing has evolved rapidly over the last few years with improvements in inkjet technology and other digital processes. One such improvement is the ability to more easily print on transparent "wraps" that can be applied to vehicles and even entire buildings—a potential extension of her company's traditional business. She knew immediately that this was the right move, and that it was within her existing set of skills and knowledge.

Although she saw her IDENTIFY moment as an exciting game changer, Soledad was aware of the risks, and of the fact that she was not in a position to start a new company. Few people are. She also had no desire to leave her current employer. So, while continuing to research the idea, she entered the final stage of the cycle.

Find a Path to NEXT

Can your mindset-shift idea (or the leapfrog moment) be carried out by your present employer or team? Will it force you to seek work elsewhere? Can you develop the idea while still performing your other duties? Are there alternatives to your initial idea that will still fulfill your aspirations?

Knowing the fiscally conservative nature of her company's executives, Soledad did not immediately propose a "moon shot" type of business expansion. Instead, she focused on how to best implement her idea as a pilot project—a leapfrog moment that involved stepping up, even at the risk of rejection or failure.

Her idea was simple. Vehicle wraps can be printed using many different wide-format devices, which were already in use for in-store retail signage. Since her retailer clients were unlikely to want to advertise on their delivery vans, she turned instead to a trade show client and proposed doing wraps for their shuttle vehicles for a large event. She sold the idea to them as a proof of concept. They agreed and were happy with the results. Throughout the process, she distinguished herself from the pack—as someone not satisfied with the grind.

The initial success led to more questions, of course. Expanding operations to include vehicle and building wraps would entail different fulfillment and installation requirements, new hires, and eventually new equipment. She would eventually be asked to lead the venture, which would mean honing her management and negotiation skills. In other words, she was using the NEXT phase to plan the GO phase of a new growth cycle.

While the Soledad example is hypothetical, the potential of growth cycles for product-oriented careers is not. Almost everyone involved in the manufacturing, handling, and sale of tangible goods can experience career growth—either within their current situation or elsewhere. Given the recent shifts in the job market, those who embrace the GAIN model will have their choice of opportunities.

Scenario #2: The Service Side

A vast segment of our economy does not produce tangible goods as their primary deliverable. But the service sector can be hard to pin down. There are pure service entities, like teaching and journalism, where the only physical evidence is a diploma or a recorded broadcast. Plumbers and electricians work with physical items, but what you pay for is their ability to make things work. Some businesses that deliver a finished physical product, like tailors and fashion designers, also provide intangible services like style and image.

Our hypothetical example in this space is an account manager—we'll call him Adam—at an advertising and public relations firm. While Adam does produce physical results, in the form of ads, press releases, and the like, his is the business of *ideas*. Adam had proven himself capable of handling the routine tasks of his initial, entry-level position in the media buying department. This led to promotion to an account management position, where diplomacy, agility, and communication skills are at a premium. Clearly, both he and those above him assumed he was good enough for the job and had the necessary skills. His potential for career growth was high, but let's take a look at how the GAIN model could accelerate that process.

Identify the GO Moment

What was the desired objective in aiming for account management? Is that still a valid goal for you?* When and how did it become clear in your mind? What made it desirable? What were the obstacles? What made you choose to go forward, despite those obstacles?

As with the first hypothetical, the best way forward was to look at the first stage. A career in advertising and PR had always suited Adam's outgoing nature. He enjoyed working with people, had a penchant for local politics, and had many of the personal qualities identified by Daniel Pink in his book *To Sell Is Human*. He was often *attuned* to and aware of others' thinking, through their words and gestures. He was also naturally *buoyant* and positive, without being afraid to confront at times, and was able to communicate with *clarity*.

To all appearances, Adam was well suited to success and would eventually grow in his chosen career. But the GAIN model would move things forward more quickly. Once he knew more about the GO part of his current growth cycle, Adam was ready to dig deeper—to expand his capabilities and learn more about his own potential. It starts with asking the right questions.

Diligently ASSESS the Current Situation

Am I in a position that excites me? Do I love advertising and PR work, or do I just enjoy the routine? Where is the industry going? How will new advertising technology affect me and my clients? What happens when big tech companies change their platforms and policies? What is the corporate ownership landscape for my industry? What are public attitudes toward advertising? Toward personal information privacy? What do I need to know about my clients? How can I relate to them more effectively?

The first question would seem to have an obvious answer given his natural abilities, but it has to be asked. Even the most outgoing advertising or PR pro can have doubts about their chosen field. But we'll stipulate that the answer to the first two questions is yes. So Adam must dig deeper. He must immerse himself in the career path he has chosen, uncover its hidden potential, and enhance his own knowledge and abilities.

Of the many service professions, advertising has undergone some of the most disruptive changes, largely due to revolutions in digital technology. The web, invented only thirty-three years ago, has changed everything related to media and advertising—a trend that has accelerated with the rise of smartphones and social media. Technologies like SEO, programmatic ad tech, and AI have flooded the industry, promising greater reach and brand engagement with less need for human-to-human interaction. Adam's assessment mandate included books ranging from classic works like *Ogilvy on Advertising* to Patrick Gilbert's *Join or Die: Digital Advertising in the Age of Automation*, and publications like *Adweek*. Added to that are uncounted web pages and blogs by ad tech and SEO gurus like Neil Patel.* To improve his people skills, Adam found advice

---

*   The SEO expert field is particularly crowded these days. Patel is one of the best known (and most prolific), but a quick search will yield such articles as "75 Top SEO Experts Worth Following in 2022," each person with a link to their respective SEO consultancy website.

from experts (in person, on TED Talks, and in books) on human psychology and engagement.

Despite his busy schedule, Adam devoted many hours to consuming this material. But he soon discovered that SEO was not a simple fix,* and that privacy concerns and tech companies' use of personal data were disrupting the ad tech field. In the midst of this unsettling discovery, he entered the third phase of the cycle.

> ## Recognize the IDENTIFY Moment
>
> During the assessment process, did an event or trend stand out as a mindset shift for you, and your role in the industry you are in? Did it resonate with you personally? Does it represent an unexpected leapfrog moment in your career— even one that may start an entirely new growth cycle? To what extent is it based on known technology or industry practices? Is there an element of fantasy or wishful thinking involved? Is it worth the time, effort, and risk involved?

Adam had always seen the value of personal connection, while also recognizing that technology was an unavoidable fact of life. During his ASSESS phase, which lasted almost four years, he discovered new platforms that could automate many of the steps involved in account management, including campaign performance and conversion rates, leaving him more time to communicate in person and enhance the relationship. In effect, he found ways to reduce the "noise" and focus on the client's needs and goals. In order to

---

* In 2020, Due North founder Ben Hirons wrote a sobering article titled, "Why This Digital Marketing Expert Says SEO Is Dead," pointing out the flaws and abuses of the practice.

become more capable as a marketer, Adam would have to learn marketing automation and data platforms that were outside his current skill set.

This IDENTIFY moment came with its own ASSESS requirements, creating a cycle within a cycle, as it were. Automation platforms are complex, especially when they involve multiple workflows. Adam did not have the expertise—or the time or budget—to implement one of these platforms on his own. So, before bringing the matter up to executives or the company's IT department, he had to know more about these platforms' capabilities. This led almost immediately to the final phase of Adam's growth cycle. It was an inflection point, where the choice was to choose between an agency or client-side role.

Find a Path to NEXT

Can your mindset-shift idea (or the leapfrog moment) be carried out by your present employer or team? Will it force you to seek work elsewhere? Can you develop the idea while still performing your other duties? Are there alternatives to your initial idea that will still fulfill your aspirations? Do you like your role in the company or the industry your company is in? This can lead to a new GO moment as you acquire new skills.

Adam's dilemma was a common one. Although his IDENTIFY moment was profound and potentially transformative, it would not easily fit into an already busy schedule. He was simply "too busy mopping the floor to turn off the faucet," as the saying goes. He was faced with three choices: He could simply forget about it and continue to juggle tasks manually. He could speak to executives or IT managers privately, to convince them to pursue it. Or he could find work with another agency that used such a platform. Adam has decided that he is a marketing and PR man and his career will be to advance in that industry, even if it means changing companies.

The leapfrog moment was pulling him toward the third option, finding a new job at a smaller, more agile agency, but it could not happen overnight. Adam's passion for direct communication also meant that his client relationships were based on trust. He could not simply leave, or try to "poach" clients for a new agency. His path to NEXT had to be taken with care.

During the following two years, Adam did everything he could to reduce the "noise" of advertising technology and focus on relationships. He simplified his own "digital footprint" by limiting the number of regular communication channels used. He advised clients to engage in campaigns with simpler, more easily measurable calls to action. Most of all, he made no secret of his IDENTIFY moment, but did not attempt to force it on his employer. When the time came to move to a smaller agency, he did so openly, with plenty of notice, and no attempts to steal clients. (Some of them followed him anyway.)

Scenario #3: Serial Entrepreneurs

Members of both product and service provider companies can benefit from the conscious application of GAIN, just as I have in the executive track. But there is another hypothetical scenario that illustrates the point. Small businesses,* entrepreneurial ones in particular, are typically started by people who regularly go through cycles of growth.

Our third hypothetical example—we'll call her Kya—is the co-founder and president of an ambitious startup company, an engineering venture pursuing the "car charging station" market. With the renewed interest in electric vehicles, her company hopes to create an improved charging device, and either license the device to existing service stations or create a franchising company to create a new type of service station.

Identify the GO Moment

What was the desired objective? Is that still a valid goal for you?* When and how did it become clear in your mind? What made it desirable? What were the obstacles? What made you choose to go forward, despite those obstacles?

Kya's graduate studies involved the challenges of electric vehicles, especially the problem of range. Although battery technology is improving, consumers are reluctant to invest in a vehicle that cannot go beyond a limited radius from the owner's home—or from a hard-to-find charging station. Slow recharge rates were also a factor, though her team believed car companies would solve that problem in relatively short order.

Her GO moment was the decision to partner with a college

---

* According to the US Chamber of Commerce, in 2022, 99.9 percent of US businesses have five hundred or fewer employees. In 2019, the Census Bureau's County Business Patterns report noted that over half of US establishments had fewer than five employees.

classmate to make a business out of their original idea: a charging station business. It was based on a prototype charger they had worked on, one that could be upgraded as new technology emerged, and could be manufactured cost effectively. The sales model was flexible, but she knew that bigger companies would soon become her greatest competitors—or her potential suitors.

Diligently ASSESS the Current Situation

Does this idea excite me?* Where is the EV industry going? How will new technology affect me and my prospective franchisees? What happens when big auto manufacturers and energy companies make similar choices? How can someone with an engineering background run a company? How will government policies and public sentiment affect my success?

Clearly, Kya has her work cut out for her. Her knowledge of the technology and where it's going is immense, but there's always something new to learn. Good business practices must be mastered, as must the competitive and regulatory factors. She can of course absorb much of this knowledge as I did, by reading books such as *The Entrepreneur's Manual*. However, in the pressure chamber of startups, there is very little time to spare. Rather than postpone her growth cycle to earn an MBA, Kya's assessment phase included bringing a savvy business partner on board and learning from their experience.

Although she had little time to read books outside her field, Kya was fortunate to have a strong network of fellow entrepreneurs. Many of these had experience on the business side, including the intricacies of raising capital and dealing with private equity firms. It was during conversations with these allies that Kya entered the third phase of her growth cycle.

Recognize the IDENTIFY Moment

During the assessment process, did something stand out as a mindset shift for you? Did it resonate with you personally?* Does it represent an unexpected leapfrog moment in your career? How will it affect not just you but also those who share your vision? Is it worth the time, effort, and risk involved?

In the tornado of activity involved in creating the new device, building the business, and seeking out capital to fund it, Kya had the thought that most startup entrepreneurs have. "Do I want to sell my company eventually or keep it and go big?" For tech companies in particular, but throughout the entrepreneurial world, dreams of a big exit—or an IPO—are common fare. We're only human, after all. We imagine what it would be like to have a big company like Google or Apple buy our idea and make us rich. It's like fantasizing about winning the lottery.

In the end, Kya and her co-founder's decision was to eventually sell the company if it became successful, but not to make that their primary objective. Sure, the money would be good for everyone involved, but she and her team were driven more by a desire for autonomy and purpose than by the carrot-and-stick approach. (She also knew that her dream could best be carried out on a large scale by a large company—one she had no desire to run.)

Kya's IDENTIFY moment was one shared by her co-founder, and

by the people committed to the idea. So, to keep the distraction of "Will so-and-so buy us out?" at bay, they consciously turned to the next phase of the growth cycle.

Find a Path to NEXT

To what extent should your mindset-shift idea (or the leapfrog moment) be carried out with your team members? How can you remain mindful of the idea while still pursuing the original GO vision? What are the actions that will accelerate and refine your original vision before the leapfrog moment occurs? What happens if that moment fails to materialize?

The prospect of a lucrative buyout is intoxicating and distracting. The history of startup companies is littered with examples of lost productivity and miscommunication caused by the prospect of venture capital. Kya and her team knew the risk, but also knew that funding was essential in order to fulfill their vision. They took steps to insulate day-to-day operations from discussions on funding rounds and business proposals. In a small company, that is difficult.

Engineering and testing went forward with as little distraction as possible. Demonstrations to potential partners and franchisees were prioritized over flashy trade events or spectacles like *Shark Tank*. Potential investors were respected and given current information, but Kya and her team refrained from future speculation whenever possible. The venture naturally attracted the interest of larger companies and competitors, but they remained patient and focused on their work.

Applying GAIN Effectively

Everyone's circumstances are different, but we all share the human desire to grow and prosper. These hypothetical examples only scratch the surface of ways that growth cycles can be applied. By asking the right questions, and digging deeper when we come up with the answers, you too can learn how to optimize the cycle of GO, ASSESS, IDENTIFY, and NEXT.

Exercise for the Reader

In this exercise, think about a significant phase of your own career. It can be an early one or something that happened much later. As you recount the events and ask the questions, be mindful of the fact that each answer is likely to require further questions and prompt you to dig deeper.

When you decided to GO for something, what was the primary objective or goal? Was it still valid and relevant as you went along? When did it become clear to you? What were the obstacles? What made you choose to go forward, despite those obstacles?

When you began, were you excited to be there? Did it engage your imagination? As you moved forward, how did you ASSESS the situation and prepare to handle it? What were your sources of information? What was within your control? What were the things outside your control? Where did you want this to go?

As you learned more about your role and became better at it, did you IDENTIFY something new that captured your imagination? How was it connected to what you had learned? Was it a natural progression or a sudden, unexpected turn? How would it impact your future path or that of the people around you?

When considering the implications of your mindset shift, how did you plan for a transition to the NEXT step? What were the barriers to proceeding immediately? Did you burn any bridges during the process? How did you manage your current responsibilities while also considering future possibilities?

BONUS QUESTIONS: How long did each of these four phases last? Were there similarities between this phase of your career and others?

Chapter 6

Overcoming Barriers to Growth

> The biggest obstacle you will ever have to overcome is your own mind!
> —**Steve Pruett**

Overcoming obstacles to growth must become a central part of your thinking if you want to create and build an extraordinary career. There will be people who embrace you and feed your desire; I call those sponsors. The other 99 percent will resist your thinking and ideas in some way or another in almost any given situation. These people aren't even necessarily being negative all the time; it is just their job to resist you. Sometimes they just don't like change. I could—and probably will—write a book focused on overcoming resistance and obstacles, as it will be a constant as you seek extraordinary growth.

In this chapter, I give you some psychology underlying resistance and how you address it. I also want you to be prepared and have a method that works for you when you encounter it. You can also refer back to the chapter on resilience and persistence for help. One particular example from my time as CEO of ComCorp stands out to me. I was originally hired in 2002 as CFO to fix CCA's capital structure. They had become overleveraged during a big acquisition spree in the 1990s. During the next four years, I restructured and replaced the entire capital stack twice.

Ultimately though, the company had no choice but to file Chapter 11. It was never in default and was performing well financially, but the debt load was just too much. Around 2008, I decided I wanted to try to lead a leveraged buyout of the company. With the permission of our PE fund Silverpoint, I began crisscrossing the country seeking financing. By 2011, I was close to giving up. I went home and told Paula I had called on forty-eight various equity investors and no one wanted to finance a TV buyout.

She paused, looked at me, and said, "Out there somewhere, someone is getting a check for their deal." I knew what that meant, and I started working on a new strategy for finding financing. That eventually led me to David Smith at Sinclair on June 20, 2011. As I stated earlier in the book, David's question to me at the end of the meeting was, "What do I need you for?" So I began working to prove to him he did need me, and on December 12, 2012, he finally agreed. While we did not get CCA, we built a nice-sized group on Chesapeake before integrating into Sinclair.

The obstacles in this process were numerous, starting with the Great Recession in 2008 when I started looking for money. But I just took them one at a time and didn't take it personally. I pivoted as needed to alternative financing strategies.

Some may be tempted to think that applying the growth principles from Part 1 is just a matter of will. For some, it may be a straightforward "just do it." Maybe they're born with the billionaire gene or the entrepreneur gene. For most of us, including myself, applying GAIN is not that simple. Because we're all too human, we create many of our own barriers to real growth.

In the GO phase of any growth cycle, there is always the danger of acting on impulse, spurred on by the instinct to act quickly, "before it's too late," or to trust that things will go well without looking at a bigger picture. But there's an equally dangerous impulse to hesitate, fearing the risk of the unknown or drawing snap conclusions from past experience. Both are barriers to real growth, and, while seemingly opposite impulses, they are both aspects of our human nature.

In 2011, Daniel Kahneman published his landmark book, *Thinking, Fast and Slow*, which introduced many to the problems of human bias and cognitive error. In a nutshell, we all tend to rely on our fast, intuitive, and emotional responses (System 1, to use his term). We are capable of slower, more deliberate, more logical responses (System 2), but we often do not exert the self-control needed to do so. This is not a moral or ethical failure. We only have so much mental bandwidth, so to speak. We exercise our System 2 reasoning when the necessity arises, putting other tasks on System 1 "autopilot," as when we drive a car on a familiar route to work.

Our reliance on automatic, System 1 thinking is the result of our evolution. Some theorize that, for example, our ancestors could imagine a dangerous animal or other threat from something they saw or heard around them. Those who reacted instinctively by running away, whether or not the threat was real, tended to survive. But when the threat *was* real, those who hesitated or failed to act swiftly perished. Thus, the tendency to see patterns and react to them unthinkingly was passed down to us by our uneaten ancestors.

This arrangement is still useful in today's complex world. With so much available information and choices before us, our inherited System 1 and 2 thinking keep us from overloading, allowing some tasks to be handled more or less automatically. But all too often our reliance on fast, System 1 thinking can result in cognitive errors—*biases*—that lead us astray. This means that, at every step of the GAIN model for growth, our biases can block our progress.

The Basics of Bias

The subject of bias has become immensely popular since Kahneman's book was published. In fact, the sheer number of unconscious biases can be overwhelming to the layman.*

It is important to examine various forms of bias in some detail here, and I would suggest some further exploration on your part because you are making some fairly serious decisions about your future when you go through the GAIN process. Bias comes in several forms, each one an attempt by our brains to process information with as little effort as possible. These mental shortcuts, while perfectly normal, can affect us adversely at almost every phase of a GAIN strategy:

The Need to Act Fast is something rooted in our primitive survival instincts. These types of bias are our brains' attempt to avoid

---

* Experts put the number of normal, human biases somewhere between 175 and 200. Searching the phrase "cognitive bias codex" will yield a bewildering diagram of 188 complex, categorized biases.

mistakes and stay focused on the immediate, relatable thing before us. It favors simple-looking options over those that seem complex or ambiguous. It also pushes us to complete the things in which we've already invested time and energy.

A strong contender in this group is the *overconfidence effect* and its close cousin, the *optimism bias*. Our confidence in our own abilities induces us to take greater risks, to make an impact, and to feel that what we do is important. And if we've had success in previous cycles, we assume, consciously or otherwise, that all will be well this time around. That's all well and good when the ASSESS phase is running smoothly and with adequate preparation. However, it can lead to disaster when all the factors are not considered.

On the opposite end from the overconfidence effect (but still in the "act fast" family) are the equally hazardous *zero-risk bias* and *loss aversion bias*. These can be powerful deterrents when considering the GO or NEXT phases of a growth cycle. Human beings love certainty—or at least the feeling of certainty—even if it is counterproductive. A certain amount of risk will always accompany any change or progress.

The "act fast" biases can also create havoc in other phases of the GAIN cycle. This includes the familiar *sunk cost fallacy*, where we attempt to justify a course of action based on the value of time and resources already spent in its pursuit. Even when evidence strongly supports going in a new direction, we feel intuitively (and mistakenly) that we ought to press on. For the aspiring entrepreneur, this can take the form of a business "pivot"—essentially a renewed attempt to justify sunk costs by redefining the same old strategy.*

---

* Not all pivot strategies are cover-ups, of course, but too many are merely attempts to save face following an expensive waste of time and resources.

Not Enough Meaning. This type of bias is pervasive throughout the business world, and can derail a growth cycle in short order. It stems from our unconscious need to find stories and patterns even when the actual data are sparse and inconclusive. To make complex ideas easier to think about, we oversimplify numbers and probabilities, such as succumbing to an artificial zero-sum choice. We also imagine people and things we're familiar with or fond of as being better or more substantial than they are.

Some of the major barriers to GAIN are in this category, including the *outcome bias*. This is when we make judgments about a past decision based on its ultimate outcome (which may be unrelated or coincidental) rather than on the quality of the decision at the time. Doing this warps the ASSESS phase of the cycle, giving people the illusion that a particular course of action is justified moving forward. Equally destructive at this stage is the *pro-innovation bias*, where we overvalue or exaggerate the benefits of a particular idea (especially one involving technology) and undervalue its limitations.

There's Too Much Information. Finally, the biggest source of barriers to growth cycles is the fact that we are inherently drawn to details that confirm what we already think. We notice things when something changes or when they are repeatedly imprinted on our memory.

Leading the pack in this group is *confirmation bias*, our relentless search for proof of things we believe. This not only limits our ability to discuss things like politics or climate change, but it also keeps us from seeing real problems during the ASSESS phase. Another gem is *choice-supportive bias*, where we naturally feel positive about a decision, like the one involved in the GO phase, but are more likely to ignore the downsides during the ASSESS phase.

The last two biases in this group are closely related. The

anchoring bias is based on our tendency to over-rely on the first piece of information received. We tend to use that initial piece of the ASSESS phase to frame the information that follows, even if the first piece was flawed in some way. This goes hand in hand with the *conservatism bias*, where we favor prior evidence or beliefs over information that emerges afterward.

To sum up, our many unconscious biases, while entirely normal, have the potential to stall the entire GAIN process. Our unconscious biases can prevent us from taking the GO step entirely, or lead to half-measures toward our personal and professional goals. They can undermine and prolong the ASSESS phase, making it ineffective or stopping it altogether.

Worst of all, by acting on unconscious assumptions or by limiting the flow of information to things we already believe, we will invariably slow or even halt our progress toward the mindset-shift moment of the IDENTIFY and NEXT phases of our journey.

The good news is that once we realize we're not alone in our stubborn humanness, we know it's possible to escape from these potential traps. The question is how. Later in the chapter, we'll look at ways to address these barriers within the GAIN model. But before we turn to remedies, let's take a closer look at some real-world examples.

Swimming with the Sharks

In 2009, Mark Burnett's reality television show *Shark Tank* premiered on ABC. A US iteration of Japan's *Dragon's Den*, the aspiring entrepreneur competition has been a critical and ratings success for fourteen seasons and counting. The formula, for those allergic to reality TV, is a series of sales pitches and demos by would-be entrepreneurs to a panel of well-known investors like Kevin O'Leary and Mark Cuban.

Part of the show's appeal is the vicarious thrill when we witness the GO moments of each contestant. Using a variety of demos and presentation antics, each person or team does their best to recreate their "aha" moment and convince at least one panelist to fund the resulting business. The sharks, with all the theatricality required for the role, play devil's advocate and ask the hard questions—on issues that should have been part of the contestant's ASSESS phase. Since the offer or refusal of investment capital is very real, both the studio and TV audiences get the thrill of watching a gladiator spectacle—without the literal bloodshed.

But besides being a brief, titillating view of the GO and ASSESS process, *Shark Tank* is an object lesson in unconscious bias. Both entrepreneurs and sharks work to counter the biases of the other side, while seeming to be blissfully unaware of their own—a textbook illustration of the bias blind spot. Presenters know that the panelists are cautious and risk averse to varying degrees, so they offer arguments loaded with confirmation and choice-supportive bias. The feedback they receive, such as "What is your business plan?" or "How will you deal with such and such problem?" are often dismissed or excused when the contestant is captivated by their own overconfidence or pro-innovation biases.

The sharks are not immune from this failing. Their GO and ASSESS decisions are based on a genuine desire to make money and/or make the world a better place and/or continue to be seen as savvy investors. They are well aware of contestants' magical thinking problem, but in the process of asking hard, ASSESS-worthy questions, they sometimes fall victim to their own biases. In one, well-publicized *Shark Tank*–related investment, Kevin O'Leary recounted how ignoring his "gut" instincts resulted in losing a half million dollars in total. After his initial $250,000 investment, he allowed his expectations and beliefs to influence how he perceived the situation—a bias known as *selective perception*. "In my stomach, I didn't feel right about it," O'Leary said. "But because I knew the guy and I liked him, and he was a friend... I gave him another [$250,000]."

Perhaps the most significant evidence of bias in *Shark Tank* is the tendency, by both contestants and panelists, to believe they see the IDENTIFY or "mindset shift" part of the cycle within a single, dramatic presentation. They may be swept up in the novelty or apparent usefulness of an idea, without having fully considered the downsides and difficulties—the *pro-innovation bias*. They may narrowly focus on an offering's most easily recognizable features—the *salience bias*, one of the hallmarks of reality TV. In other words, both entrepreneurs and sharks are forced by the nature and format of the show to compress what is naturally a years-long growth cycle process. With too much information to process in so short a time, our System 1 shortcuts step in, with unconscious bias affecting the results. In the non-television world, innovation and growth can take a different path, especially if we guard against unconscious assumptions.

Dangerous Assumptions

In Chapter 3, I briefly recounted my misadventures as an auto parts business owner. One of the many things I learned from this experience, and the resulting financial crash, was the unfortunate power of my own unconscious assumptions. My biases included overconfidence in my own ability and the positive feelings I had about my choice, despite its flaws. I failed to adequately research and understand the prevailing business model and its limitations to combat a shift in competition.

The problem began with my GO moment, or rather with my reason for making such a choice. To be honest, I simply loved cars, as I still do. I loved everything about them. I thought, "I've been successful financing and running media companies. Why couldn't I apply those skills and experience to something else I really love?" Without more careful consideration, I proceeded to invest my own money in an auto parts business. As I related earlier, it was a disaster.

During what should have been a more objective ASSESS phase, I neglected some basic facts. For one thing, I didn't carefully examine the typical business plan of this type of operation. If I had pushed beyond my own biased opinions, I would have discovered more. Even the people selling me the company said things that should have been warning signs. They told me the business was all about the little things, like knowing and managing prices and inventory in relentless detail. I knew that CEOs of major chains like AutoZone and NAPA must have "had people to handle those things," but I was less concerned about doing that myself. That was a big mistake, especially for someone just starting out.

That particular ostrich effect had another, more serious implication. During the GO and ASSESS phases, I never asked myself if I would truly enjoy running this type of business. As it turned out, my love of cars was not synonymous with the daily grind of running a parts business—or even a small chain of such stores. I let my belief that I was an entrepreneurial genius (which I'm not) and my love of cars direct my search for facts to support those beliefs.

One positive that came out of my failure was that I became

obsessed with understanding business models in a real sense, which became a super power of mine and facilitated much of my growth for the rest of my career. Failure, and understanding the failure, led to success.

These kinds of false assumptions are common, whether you're a budding entrepreneur, a one-person service provider, or an employee with big ideas for your company. An aspiring photographer may have visions of dramatic photo shoots in the Amazon jungle, but not of taking kids' photos at Walmart. An architect may think about creating the next exotic resort, but not about the parking structure for a new shopping mall. You cannot let your expectations of an ideal outcome be the basis for your GO decision. You have to look at the full spectrum of possible outcomes, with the "ideal" ranked as a low probability. Then ask yourself if you'd be satisfied with success at a less-than-perfect level.

If the answer is no, then your ASSESS process needs to switch gears, so to speak. It must either find new ways to put your current growth cycle back on track or else make you open to a different leapfrog moment, and a different GO.

Planning for Success

Some barriers to your growth are put there by circumstances outside your control, or by the biases and prejudices of others. This applies whether you're working on your own career or starting a business. There's not much you can do to change these, apart from finding a new growth cycle that meets your needs. But many of the barriers to growth are self-generated, rooted in your own assumptions and biases. To overcome these, you need a plan.

First, always acknowledge that your initial GO was very likely affected by some (or a lot) of unconscious bias on your part. False assumptions and cognitive errors are not easy to spot in yourself, so *it's usually best to have honest conversations with those you trust, and actually listen to the answers*. (Later in the book, we'll talk about the vital role of coaches and other genuine influencers—not the manufactured kind.)

Discovering your biases may not prove fatal to your current growth cycle, but knowing them will certainly inform your ASSESS phase, and make it more likely you will get to IDENTIFY and NEXT in less time. In fact, discovering a previously hidden bias can often lead to its own leapfrog moment, leading in turn to an entirely new and more satisfying growth cycle.

In the early stages of a cycle, and preferably before the cycle begins, always put your personal desires and fantasies aside (or at least write them down) before planning your next move. This will help you gain some perspective and put a damper on your System 1 impulses. For every best-case scenario you can think of in your current cycle, always think up three or more "next-best" cases. These can even include results you could reasonable live with, knowing that future growth cycles are always possible.

An important part of your plan must include an honest answer to two questions: "What does success look like?" and "Do I really want that?" Even if "success" is less than your imagined ideal, you must be not only willing to tolerate it but also reasonably happy doing it. Without that understanding, your cycle will eventually grind to a halt. When I started my investment banking career, all I saw was a need I knew I could fill—a gap in growth financing for broadcasters. It was something I had learned from my previous experience, and, more importantly, it was something I knew I would enjoy doing on a larger scale.

Bias and false assumptions can affect every aspect of a growth cycle. Fear of taking risks can prevent you from even starting on a new path. Unfounded beliefs and assumptions can derail the assessment process, making it take far longer than necessary, and preventing you from gaining vital information. Worse still, they can prevent you from reaching a genuine mind-shift moment, that realization of where your journey will go next.

Exercise for the Reader

In this exercise, think about the growth cycle you are currently in, no matter which phase of GAIN applies right now. List all the barriers you can think of, both in yourself and coming from others, and practical steps to overcome them. As you think about these barriers, consider the following questions:

1. What are the biases I can observe *in others* that are preventing them from seeing or acting on my ideas? As you list these errors (the ostrich effect, anchoring, conservatism, risk or loss aversion, overconfidence, confirmation bias, sunk cost fallacy, etc.), ask if any of them apply to *you*.
2. What is standing in the way of the GO or NEXT phase of your current growth cycle? Are you unduly averse to possible risk or loss? Are past assumptions or beliefs

taking priority over new information? In your mind, does a recent, unpleasant experience outweigh good ones in the past?

3. Is your ASSESS process free from unconscious, biased assumptions? Are you seeking out evidence to support what you already believe? Are you ignoring dangerous or negative information? Do you have an inflated view of your own judgment or abilities? Do you believe you've invested time or resources that would be wasted if you changed course?

4. If you've reached the IDENTIFY phase, have you looked at the "big idea" from more than one angle? Can you set aside your personal desire when considering it? Have you examined the business model and other practical aspects of the idea? What does success look like? Would you be truly happy doing that, no matter what its level of success?

5. After asking and answering these questions, are you still committed to this particular cycle? Is it worth your time and continued effort? Does a change of direction mean failure? Are you open to the possibility of a leapfrog moment that would overrule your current growth cycle?

Chapter 7

Influencers

> Attach to the best of positive people
> and make them a long-term part of your being.
> —**Steve Pruett**

There will be people in your life who will take an interest in you and be in a position to influence you. Some of it will be positive. Some of it will be negative. Most of it will be somewhere in between. Take what you need, because both kinds of influence will impact your trajectory.

This chapter is so important that it was very difficult for me to decide what form it should take. I wanted to mention specific influencers for me, but I decided that after I identified north of a thousand, I couldn't do it without leaving people out. I could write an entire book and name names and define what they did, and maybe I will. Instead, for now, I made a list of the types of influencers.

The number one influencer is people. The direct influence of people, whether positive or negative, will make you. People can't break you; only you can break you. I have had people say one paragraph or one sentence to me that made a huge impact on my career. I absorbed that help and used it as fuel for the fire that drove me. I have had people believe in me, invest money in me, and more importantly, invest time in me.

I have also had people block me, badmouth me, attack me, cheat me, mislead me, and manipulate me. But I used those things to get stronger and wiser.

In the rest of this chapter, I talk about reading and research. These are key tools of influence, whether movies, TV shows, documentaries, fiction, nonfiction, biographies, you name it. The more you absorb from a wide variety of sources, the more thorough your perspective of the world will be. If you take all this in, you should be able to form your own conclusions about what it means to you and your path.

Don't isolate yourself in an echo chamber of your industry, politics, or social circle. Look at everything, including history (the factual kind, not the opinion kind). This is your life, and any tool that gives you the ability to circulate and get along with a wide range of people will be instrumental in your development.

Throughout my career, many people have directly influenced my views on life, some by example and many who wanted to help me grow as a person or businessman. Influence can be a potent agent for bad outcomes at least as often as good ones. The trouble is, although we think ourselves capable of separating the two, we often fail to recognize who our influencers are, much less how their words and actions impact our growth.

Influence is critical to the GAIN process. Seeking, finding, and following positive and constructive influence is a major factor in accelerating the growth process. But the real challenge is separating good influence from bad. Negative influence can be hidden and indirect, derailing our growth, sometimes permanently.

When you hear the word *influencer* today, you're likely to think of someone on TikTok or Instagram giving you their latest take on something, in a more or less entertaining fashion, and asking you to Like or Follow them. There's more to it than that, of course. According to a claim by the Danish publication, *Influencer MarketingHub*, founded way back in 2016, businesses can make a $5.78 return on investment for every dollar spent on influencer marketing. That curiously specific ROI number is not the issue. The real problem is the confusion today's marketing gurus and social media personalities create over the words *influencer* and *influence*.

Influence is as old as mankind. We are social animals, naturally attuned to the other members of our tribe. To survive and thrive, our ancestors took their cues from others. When their responses had a positive outcome, other members of the tribe aspired to the status of *giving* those cues and having them followed. Today we are pretty much the same. To paraphrase Dale Carnegie, part of the modern human condition is our quest to win friends and influence people.

For our purposes, however, let's take a closer look at what influence really is, how to find it, and how to distinguish true influence from the *manufactured* variety—which is 90 percent of the media noise that bombards you every day. More importantly, let's consider how to receive and process that influence to our own advantage, using the GAIN model to fuel your own growth cycles.

Back to Basics

The *Cambridge Dictionary* defines influence as "the power to have an effect on people or things, or a person or thing that is able to do this." In its simplest form, it is a collection of words and/or actions that have some noticeable effect on our attitudes and behaviors. The words can be spoken or written, live or recorded, explicit or subtle, combined with imagery or left to stand on their own. The actions can range from subtle body language to conduct observed over a long period of time. They can be the actions of an actual person you know or a fictional character in a book or movie. *Influence is anything that reaches one or more of our senses, resonates with our thoughts and emotions, and triggers a response—hopefully a positive one.* Good influencers are people with whom we can identify, and who embody our values and goals. Influence is the "spark" (usually one of many) that changes the course of our lives. I am not going to try to impart a psychological analysis of influence and spend a lot of time recognizing it as a key component of your journey. It is critical, however, to become adept at separating the positive and negative effects of influence.

Rather than get sucked into that whirlpool, I'd rather just state a layman's opinion: *We are all influenced by our surroundings*, whether we know it or not, and whether or not we have inherited genes that make us more or less likely to act responsibly.

In addition to our physical and social surroundings, we are also influenced by the value we assign to a particular task, and the mood or perception that value creates. If the action before us meets a need—everything from physiological needs like eating and breathing to the "higher" needs like security and a sense of belonging—it becomes easier to pursue.

The point of describing situational influence is not to prepare you for a debate, but to help you read the room more accurately, or move to a different room when necessary. I have worked with hundreds of people and situations over the course of my career. At times, I can trace my personal inflection points and leapfrog moments to a specific individual or situation, but more often than not, their influence is far more subtle.

Recognizing the Sources of Influence

Both Pink and Cialdini—and a host of other writers and TED Talkers—are adept at describing the most visible manifestation of intentional and situational influence: sales and salespeople. But focusing on those influencers limits the scope of possibilities. Influence and influencers can take many forms, so they can be hard to identify as such. You must know how to find them, separate the "manufactured" aspects of their influence from the real thing, and above all allow the right influence in. Here are some of the possibilities:

Direct Interaction with a Person. This is the most basic source of influence, intentional or otherwise. In my experience, direct interaction with people is the most impactful and important form of influence, whether intentional or incidental. There will be people who influence for three minutes and others who will be an influencer for your entire career. Some will be positive and some will be negative; they all have value. It begins with family members and people in your school or other social setting, which can be either good or bad. My own interaction with Grandmother, for example, was an overwhelmingly positive influence, but one outside my control. As we grow up, our interactions tend to be more deliberate, based on how a person's ideas or attributes resonate with us and our ideals and goals. Ideally, the influence derived from these interactions is mutual, as it should be with friends and true colleagues. If the relationship is imbalanced in some way, as with an employer and employee, the influence is likely to flow in one direction, but in my experience it still goes both ways.

Even "non-ideal" situations can be sources of good influence. For example, my old sales manager, Manny, was a prickly, no-nonsense individual with little or no desire to spare my feelings. Even now, I find it hard to visualize a collegial relationship with someone like him. But the fact was that he influenced my growth cycle at a young age, which has positive echoes to this day. Many of you probably recall having a teacher or a sports coach who gave you a particularly hard time, and who you undoubtedly irritated in return. It could also be someone who simply makes you feel uncomfortable, intentionally or not. Looking back, however, you'll probably consider that person a pivotal influence in your life, no matter how well or how poorly it all ended.

Teachers and coaches are only two of the many types of individuals whose influence is intentional (and also paid for, by the way). The list includes doctors, attorneys, therapists, business coaches, ministers, inspirational speakers, and many others. This does not automatically mean that their influence is good for you. As is the case with some advertising, a professional you experience in person can also offer what I call "manufactured" influence (i.e., words or actions designed to achieve *their* ends, not yours). Even when their words or actions resonate with you, the trick is to examine that influence objectively, without becoming overly skeptical. This is part of the ASSESS process described in Chapter 1.

Of course, the majority of our influential interactions with people are not planned, scheduled, or paid for, other than the time we invest in each relationship. I'm referring to the many people we interact with during the course of our personal and professional lives. These interactions can be intense and long lasting or they can be completely casual. An offhand remark ("Have you thought of such and such?") can just as easily be an inflection point for you as can a highly focused conversation. It need not even be expressed in words. A colleague's actions and choices, if they are willing to share them, can speak volumes.

If you're lucky and I was very lucky, some people of import and influence will believe in you enough to effectively invest their time, money, and influence in you simply because they see something promising or they think you can add to their own mission. As I will detail later in this chapter, some of those people will be with you for decades.

In earlier chapters, I shared a part of my history with two individuals who have affected my journey: Phil McGraw and Mark Burnett. Our relationship was collegial. Neither provided explicit, intentional influence, although both are qualified to do so. Both men influenced me—and my understanding of growth cycles—but in completely different ways.

Phil's example was more of a deliberately planned path. He went to college with the intent to play football (among other things). As circumstances changed, he adjusted his path accordingly, going into psychology and eventually broadcasting. Mark's example was closer to my own. Knowing he just couldn't stand it if he stayed bound to a manufacturing job, he made an abrupt choice to join the Royal Marines. There and afterward, he experienced various inflection points that led him to his current role as an influential television producer. Both examples resonated with me and embodied different versions of GAIN, long before I knew what that even was.

The problem with in-person interactions, as plentiful as they are, is that they are only a small sample of a much larger pool of potential influence. Fortunately, there is a way to interact with that wider world, and seek out the influence that will accelerate your growth cycles:

Indirect Interaction with a Person's Words and Ideas. I have been a voracious reader all my adult life, as my boxes, shelves, and e-readers full of books will attest. Through these and other sources of the written word, I have "met" and been influenced by individuals long dead and far outside my circle. We cannot underestimate its importance as a source of influence.

There are of course nonfiction books beyond count advocating best practices and systems for leadership success and career advancement. Nearly all of them constitute intentional influence, and many are well worth the time required to read them. But the sheer number of these books can be daunting. So, rather than provide a list of *my* recommended nonfiction books, I'll suggest a more GAIN-centric approach: *Evaluate a book and its potential influence value the same way you would evaluate its author if you met them in person.* Read the cover summary or a few pages on its Amazon or Goodreads page, and perhaps a qualified review or two, and ask these questions:

- Does the book's practical, clearly stated theme or message resonate with me personally?
- Does it relate to any of the four phases of GAIN?
- Does it hold the promise of a mindset shift or a leapfrog moment in a new or unexpected direction?

Reading, listening to audiobooks and podcasts, and watching videos that address your development are all ways to take in relevant information, as long as you feel the creators are legitimately qualified on the subject. A book must earn its place in your repertoire of knowledge. There is no penalty for *not* finishing a book once you realize the author is not fulfilling the book's initial promise. Donating a book to Goodwill, or just recycling it, can be just as meaningful in your ASSESS process as the act of giving it an honored place on your bookshelf.

There are also multiple ways to experience a book, including the audio version and the space-saving e-book. But keep in mind that such convenience comes with a cost. A 2013 study* found that students who read text in printed form had significantly greater comprehension of the material than students who read it on screen. At the risk of sounding old fashioned, the experience of reading something on paper—something involving touch as well as sight—is simply more memorable and impactful than doing so on a screen, especially a screen that has built-in distractions.

Books are of course not the only way to discover the mind of a potential influencer. Like most of us, you have access to an overabundance of articles, white papers, and summaries, filling your inbox and clamoring for your limited attention. To manage the flood and make it meaningful to your growth cycle, you need to apply the same screening questions as you would with books. Remember that you are vetting the author themselves as well as the quality and relevance of their ideas.

By now, you have a good idea about my penchant for connecting

---

* Mangen, Walgermo, and Brønnick, "Reading Linear Texts on Paper versus Computer Screen: Effects on Reading Comprehension," *International Journal of Educational Research 58* (2013): 61–68.

with influencers via their written words. But nonfiction "business principles" books only scratch the surface when it comes to influence. Knowing about their actions and decisions is at least as important as reading their words and absorbing their ideas. But the chances of meeting such people in person are small. If you cannot transport yourself or travel back in time to find influential leaders, the next best thing is to seek out insightful biographies.

Two of my favorite influencers are George Washington and Abraham Lincoln. Biographies of both are plentiful, but I recommend Ron Chernow's Pulitzer Prize–winning *Washington: A Life* and Doris Kearns Goodwin's *Team of Rivals: The Political Genius of Abraham Lincoln*. Both men faced insurmountable problems and chaotic, contradictory opposition, often from among their own ranks. I found that both men epitomized the ideas of GO and ASSESS at each stage of their political careers, as Washington did in his military career. Both were able to IDENTIFY the correct but unexpected move. Naturally, there is more to each of their stories, but the only way to gain insight into their lives, and to apply those insights into our own cycles, is to read about them. The skill of the biographers is key here. They must tell the story with the least bias possible, but also unearth facets of the subject's life that resonate, illustrate sound principles of growth and change, and reveal new or unexpected insights under difficult circumstances.

Aside from works of pure propaganda, no honest biography will ignore the weaknesses or failures of its subject. The lives of Washington and Lincoln are no exception. Even though their character and outcomes were far from perfect, I have found that their pursuit of growth and their willingness to embrace unexpected courses of action are reasons to receive and incorporate their influence. I have since perused other biographies with the same thought, not simply to reinforce my own beliefs, but also to check my beliefs against what others have done.

No list of influential words and actions would be complete without including fiction and storytelling. In their oral, written, and performed modes, stories are among mankind's oldest forms of communicating abstract ideas. They are intentional in nature, conceived in the mind of the storyteller, and presented in a way designed to reinforce or challenge the beliefs influencing one's thinking and decision-making on all levels.

The power and purpose of fiction was expressed in a nutshell by Pulitzer Prize–winning essayist Annie Dillard in her 1982 masterpiece, *Living by Fiction*:

> Fiction can deal with all the world's objects and ideas together, with the breadth of human experience in time and space; it can deal with things the limited disciplines of thought either ignore completely or destroy by methodological caution, our most pressing concerns: personality, family, death, love, time, spirit, goodness, evil, destiny, beauty, will. Fiction writers are, I hope to show, thoughtful interpreters of the world.

I would go as far as to say that without the influence of fiction and storytelling our desire and capacity to grow would be purely mechanical, a behavioristic response to stimulus—promises of reward or threats of punishment. Personally, I recoil at the thought. The *reason* I pursue my own growth cycles with conviction (and persuade others to do so) is not to earn a few more dollars, or to avoid earning less. The former is a likely result, but the real reason I do all this is to satisfy my heart's desire, that inner force that is best expressed in story. It can be firsthand stories, like my life with Grandmother or my encounters with Phil, Mark, or Manny, but it also can be with people who only exist in a writer's imagination—and in yours.

There's one advantage that fiction has over nonfiction books and articles. Reading the latter can feel like homework, even if you have excellent sources and a clear idea of what you're seeking. Novels and short stories, on the other hand, do not (or should not) impose on your personal preferences. All they ask for is time, and all they promise is enjoyment. You may prefer fantasy, science fiction, mystery, historical fiction, horror, romance, or any other genre. You may prefer conventional or graphic novels, short stories or epics, any mix of words and ideas that resonates—it does not matter. It helps to occasionally venture outside your comfort zone, but good influence can be found in books that you already love.

Of course, a good book is not a guarantor of good, constructive influence. One can always take the wrong message from any written work, just as from interacting with the influencer in person. But the same filtering process applies:

- Do the words and actions resonate with me and my driving purpose?
- Am I viewing them through my own biases and preconceptions, or am I seeing them in their full context?

- Do they relate in a constructive way to the GO, ASSESS, IDENTIFY, or NEXT phases of my current growth cycle?
- Do they provide or point out an unexpected leapfrog moment that would lead me in a different direction?

Interaction through the Lens of Media. So far, I've talked about influence as it pertains to interaction with a live person or their written words. But today there is an entirely different aspect of both. Thanks to the "miracle" of film, radio, television, and their newer internet counterparts, influence now has a host of new channels vying for our time and attention.

To understand the effectiveness of this kind of influence, remember that humans relied on sights and sounds (and to a lesser extent feelings, smells, and tastes) before we had words to describe them—and *way* before we could read and write those words. As we found ways to mass produce and deliver visual and audible messages, we discovered that they were a powerful and more focused means of influencing others, without the need to write words and try to make them understood.

This "lens of media," while relatively new, is not fundamentally different from other forms of influence. It can be a narrative heard on a podcast (which is, of course, radio via the internet); it can be streaming video (movies or television shows via the internet); or it can be an audio playlist (a custom album via the internet). It can be pure fiction or the words of a teacher, journalist, or public speaker. The point is that, just like the actions and written words of any would-be influencer, they can and should be filtered with the same questions and embraced or rejected to the extent that they support your growth cycle.

In 1992, the grunge rock group Soundgarden released the song "Rusty Cage" on their studio album *Badmotorfinger*. Four years later, Johnny Cash released his own version of the song, expressing the same feelings that "I'm gonna break my rusty cage and run" with a tough, country vibe. Both versions resonated with me at a time in my career when I was dissatisfied, to say the least, with corporate inertia and bureaucracy. I did not take the song as some mysterious message to uproot my life and become a rebel. But it did play a part in my ASSESS phase, as I re-examined a previous GO decision. Ultimately, it became part of the emotional fabric that influenced my leapfrog moment, and my decision to take my NEXT step in my career.

Influence conveyed through the media lens can be scary at times, thanks in part to its potential for abuse. Algorithm-driven social media is a case in point. Many platforms are loaded with examples of influence turned to bad ends, reflecting the old saying, "A lie can travel halfway around the world before the truth can get its boots on." But just because a medium can be abused does not mean it should be ignored. As our channels of influence multiply, it is more important than ever to look at them in context and consider their influence for their intrinsic value—or lack thereof.

Influence and Growth Cycles

Influence, from whatever source, poses two fundamental requirements. It must be *evaluated*, as described in the previous section, for resonance, possible bias, and applicability to one's current situation. More importantly, positive influence must be *incorporated* into your own life and growth cycles. The best examples and counsel on the planet will be absolutely useless if they are not acted upon and put to good, practical use.

Good influence is especially important at the GO phase. Early on, the drive to seize upon a new path or opportunity can be reckless and potentially dangerous, as was my dash to "catch" Grandmother as she drove away. Her personal influence was part of that decision, to be sure, but other influences (motivation, acceptance, safety, courage, overcoming fear, drive, etc.) were also at work, channeling my impulsive move into more productive channels as time went on. With each successive GO, the positive influence of other people, their words, and the words and stories of our imaginations will make your initial move more decisive, more grounded in the real world, and less likely to explode on the runway.

The ASSESS phase is where influence has the greatest overall impact. As you become experienced in detecting genuine, positive influence, as opposed to the manufactured kind, you will become better equipped to take that influence and act upon it. Think of it in terms of building blocks, or stepping stones, or tools for creating something new. What was only an aspiration during the GO stage can become a working reality as you incorporate those things in the ASSESS stage. Similarly, influence is crucial in getting to IDENTIFY, the mindset shift that affirms your previous choices and clarifies the "one thing" you will pursue NEXT.

Speaking of the NEXT phase, this is potentially the time when you can turn your influence and experience to the benefit of others. As you work toward a positive outcome for yourself *and* those you'll be leaving, your actions and words can in turn influence others in their respective growth cycles.

Finally, one of the greatest outcomes stemming from genuine, positive influence is the potential to identify leapfrog moments—those unexpected insights that can lead you to GO in a new direction altogether. It can come from interaction with a trusted colleague or mentor, to be sure, or from written or recorded words from a reliable source. But very often leapfrog moments and insights can come "out of the blue" from a novel or a television show that resonates with you personally and with the "fire" that prompted your initial GO moment.

Influence is indeed all around us, and we contribute our share, consciously or not. What we do with it, in terms of growth cycles, is the subject of our final chapter.

Exercise for the Reader

In this exercise, write down your top ten influencers, either from a significant time in your past or in your present situation. For each influencer, note the following:

1. Is the influencer someone with whom you interact (or interacted) in person or indirectly, through books, articles, or other media?
2. Write down as many inflection points or leapfrog moments you associate with this influencer. Be as detailed as you like to help you build an accurate picture of that person's influence.

3. What did you do to incorporate that influence in a growth cycle? How did it affect your decision to GO, ASSESS, IDENTIFY, and/or proceed to NEXT?
4. How did you use that experience to influence others in your personal or professional circle?

Chapter 8

Making Growth Cycles Your Own

> Start early and find some magic dust
> that differentiates you from others.
> —**Michael W. Kublin, president, PeopleTek Inc.**

One of Warren Buffett's remarkable achievements is that he has generated over 90 percent of his wealth since he turned sixty-five years old. This reflects his approach of "getting rich slow," which was a response he is said to have given Amazon.com Chairman Jeff Bezos. Experience and skills compound similar to money in investments. It is important to get started early and be disciplined in acquiring them through education, hard work, and taking on responsibility. There is no greater motivator than being responsible for other people, especially loved ones.

When I first began to formulate ideas about growth cycles, I thought a lot about the *mechanics*. I explored what was involved in deciding to GO for something, ASSESS the many aspects and consequences of that decision, IDENTIFY the unexpected but significant mindset shift, and embrace the NEXT stage with intelligence and empathy. Equally important, however, is the *timing* of our own growth cycles.

In her popular 2013 TED Talk,* psychologist and author Meg Jay argued that people in their twenties are the ideal age to acquire "identity capital" and the means of attaining exponential growth in their later life and careers. Contrary to popular myth, she asserted that our twenties are not "developmental downtime." They are the time when building one's positive character and habits will have the greatest long-term results. "Claiming your twenties," Jay said, "is one of the simplest, yet most transformative things you can do." Start early and stay with it, but assess and make opportunistic pivots.

The same principle holds true for developing the habits involving growth cycles. Thankfully, GAIN can be successfully applied by anyone at any time in their careers. However, like Buffett's compounding approach to investing, the effects of GAIN are greater when applied early on. To paraphrase Dr. Jay, *when you explore and do things that add value to who you are, that is an investment in who you might want to become.*

This also applies to leapfrog moments, those unexpected opportunities or thoughts that can fundamentally change a material outcome or the current direction or path you are on. As we

---

* Meg Jay, "Why 30 Is Not the New 20," 2013, TED video, https://www.ted.com/talks/meg_jay_why_30_is_not_the_new_20.

discussed in Chapter 2, leapfrog moments can be life-changing, aha epiphanies that you tell your grandkids about one day. But they can also be small, "mini-leapfrog moments." These are actually easier to take advantage of early on. When they happen, and you take advantage of the opportunity, leapfrog moments of any size have a compounding effect—paying dividends, as it were—when it comes to your subsequent growth cycles.

In my late teens and early twenties, I worked at a variety of odd, mostly boring jobs. One was with a company that designed and sold industrial heating systems—a very staid firm, like Dunder Mifflin in the U.S. version of *The Office*. I had "graduated" from working in the warehouse to being a lowly paper pusher, when I noticed that the sales engineers really hated working with smaller customers. They hated doing the calculations for small projects, even though the math was simple—or maybe because it *was* so simple and tedious. Even though I wasn't a math wizard or an engineer, I offered to learn the math and take on the jobs nobody wanted to do, but, in particular, I helped the one outside salesperson. This salesperson was overwhelmed with work and needed help to service customers.

It was a miniature leapfrog moment. When I began picking up the tasks others didn't want, I got on the company owner's radar, to the extent that he offered to help fund my education if I stayed on. From that point, finding things that others didn't want to do became my MO, eventually developing into a habit, leading to a series of mini-leapfrog moments throughout my early career. Being the person that would take on extra work beyond my lane became a major leveraging point for me to this day.

The habit compounded over time. As a young television ad salesperson, I saw that there were many tasks people just didn't like, or were too busy to do in the time available. Ultimately, by personally taking every step to process my orders, I learned how the entire TV station functioned and who was in charge of each department. That is how I figured out my first TV station business plan. I was able to leapfrog from salesperson to station partner because I raised investment based on that plan. Because I showed I could implement a plan, no one really questioned my background. A version of that can still work today as new and unknown technologies are emerging where existing expertise in applications is thin.

When an ad had to be produced and the creative team's schedule was full, I would find out how to produce the content myself. I also saw that the traffic department, where TV ads are scheduled, was a hectic and stress-filled part of the station, so I went there.* In those days, television ads had to be manually assigned to specified time slots, so I asked if there were any empty slots at the end of a broadcast cycle. Of course there were, so I asked my client if they cared when every ad was played. Since they wanted greater coverage without going over on cost, they agreed, and the account grew to be one of the station's biggest.†

Each time I sought out a task that was outside my "normal" routine, usually one that others didn't care to do, I opened the door

---

* These days, salespeople are not allowed to go to traffic directly, for fear they will "jump the line" by scheduling their own ads, but I was the new guy, and it was the '70s.

† This approach is called remnant advertising—now very common in the media world. It is also known by its algorithmically driven name, "programmatic advertising." I certainly didn't invent it, but by exploiting people's aversion to tedious work, I experienced a leapfrog moment.

for another leapfrog moment. Each one had a compounding effect. Most were seemingly small at the time, but each one gave me a new place to GO and ASSESS, leading occasionally to a breakthrough IDENTIFY and NEXT moment. And because I ingrained the habit of making these leaps as a younger man, I found it easier to do later.

Everyone Is the Same—and Different

I believe the GAIN process can be applied to any career, at any time—with early application resulting in greater, compounding benefits. It is also applicable to life in general. I base this belief on the fact that we as humans have an innate desire to do something more than a routine, day-to-day job, punctuated by random leisure activities. The pandemic-fueled Great Resignation was an object lesson. All humans want more than a paycheck for doing eight hours of daily work, especially when the work has little intrinsic meaning. As Abraham Maslow theorized, our needs are more complex than food, shelter, and safety. We all have higher needs that drive us forward—in different ways and with different cycles of growth.

One way to prove this is to look at how we actually spend our leisure time. While many leisure activities may seem pointless, breaks in a dull routine, they can also reveal a lot about a person's higher needs. Sometimes the need is to do something transcendent and altruistic, like doctors who devote their spare time to helping treat disease in poor or underserved communities. For others, it is mainly an extension of their own passion, like the car mechanic who works on antique car restoration just for fun, or on fixing cars for someone less fortunate. There are so many other ways to spend leisure time, some obviously meaningful and others selfish to everyone but the person doing it. In every case, the activity is a clue to that person's higher needs, and their reason to seek a way to grow.

This is a helpful clue in revealing the GO phase of your next growth cycle. When something resonates enough to warrant spending your free time on it, chances are you'll be looking for reasons to do it more often. Eventually, you'll find a way to do it that involves a career shift, large or small, toward a job that meets your true needs. That same passion will fuel the ASSESS process, to confirm or modify your trajectory. It will also give you the context for recognizing the IDENTIFY moment when it happens. And of course it will prepare you (and hopefully those around you) for the NEXT stage of your driving passion.

None of us can or should try to follow the exact same career path, and of course no one is guaranteed a successful outcome or the fulfillment of every dream. But we each have the potential to achieve career and personal growth. We can each find our respective growth cycles by paying attention to our interests and passions—the things that truly satisfy us. If we do, we may even help those around us achieve their own growth cycles.

Asking Good Questions

Finding the motivation to consciously pursue GAIN is not terribly difficult. The first symptom is *restlessness*, a feeling that your current work situation is all bound up and not moving forward in the way you want it to. At this point, the question to ask is, "Why do I feel this way?" followed by, "What is in the way of getting to the place I want to be?"

If the answers are not obvious, then you'll need to dig deeper. Dissatisfaction alone will not do much to get a growth cycle moving.

It takes a measure of courage, thoughtfulness, and willingness to take risks, knowing that failure is always possible. It also takes transparency, honesty (with yourself and others), and persistence. This is the time when the right kind of influencers can make a big difference, as we discussed in the last chapter.

The more you experience growth cycles, the easier it will become to recognize the steps. GO is simply the urge to pursue the knowledge or activity that you find interesting or enjoyable. It doesn't matter if it is your work, an avocation, or simply the necessity of earning more money—enough to meet your basic needs. ASSESS arrives as you think about what this activity means to you, what you're exchanging in time and effort, and whether you believe it's worth it. This last part is extremely personal, of course, and can only be decided by the person doing the assessment.

Some not-so-hypothetical statements and questions may prove helpful. You may find yourself saying, "I don't want to volunteer at the church/school/food bank anymore because it isn't doing as much good as I think it can." This is an ASSESS statement. Follow that with the right questions: Is there a way to make my time more consistent or rewarding? Where can my time be put to better use? Can I get results some other way or at some other organization doing similar work? Moving on to the assessment mode is the next step in the GAIN process, where you can begin to search for options and IDENTIFY your new NEXT.

Here's another example. If you say, "At work, I've been going above and beyond for a year, but I'm not getting rewarded in a way that meets my actual needs." This is another assessment, so explore what happens when you follow that feeling with more questions: Would I be more fulfilled if I had my boss's job, or their boss's job? Would more money and responsibility make me feel fulfilled? Would

I feel fulfilled with something else entirely? Where and how can I achieve that goal?

If you ask yourself questions about *why* you don't feel rewarded, despite your extra effort, it will help you identify *what* is keeping you from moving forward. As you do this, you'll move on to the IDENTIFY stage. In fact, the normal pattern is to move back and forth between IDENTIFY and ASSESS as you get closer to the answer of what the NEXT step will be. The answers may surprise you.

Everything to Gain

The GO phase of a growth cycle can be easy to recognize, especially as such opportunities occur so regularly. The feelings of longing, reflection, and realization naturally pop up throughout your career, your personal life, or both at once. They can spring from something you read, hear, or watch. They may spring from interactions with influencers, or they may come seemingly out of nowhere. Even as our routinized work and media culture tends to create conformity and process for its own sake, something in us seems to chafe at the restrictions and seeks a new path, often from childhood on. When the logical GO options are limited, we leapfrog, skipping entire assignments or career steps to pursue a trajectory that will actually be fulfilling.

GO is clearly the most important action, as it both begins and ends a cycle. In fact, after the first cycle you've consciously applied, GO and NEXT are closely related, if not interchangeable. NEXT implies or precedes a GO event. Similarly, ASSESS is the act of measuring your *most recent* GO event, while IDENTIFY reveals the growth cycle that follows logically (or not so logically, if it's a leapfrog).

Deciding to GO can be simple or complex. Very often, that depends on where you are, timing- and development-wise. If you are just out of school, and at a natural beginning of a career path, then choosing a goal can be as simple as getting an entry-level job in your chosen field of study. (After all, before you entered school or a training program of any kind, you hopefully made a GO decision to study a specific field.) But it's not always that simple. You may take a job regardless of the field, for purely economic reasons—or just to enter the workforce to learn what it's all about.

Regardless of the reason, after you've made the leap, you will spend the next several weeks or months immersing yourself in the new challenges and duties involved. At some point, you will also take a moment or two to reflect on your progress. Even if you are ecstatic about how things are going, this is the first time you will really ASSESS your most recent GO moment. This will likely spur you on to greater engagement and cause you to dive even deeper into your new environment. You'll begin to see pathways to your obvious (and not-so-obvious) goals. As the ASSESS phase continues, these turn into roads and highways that begin to form a map of where your initial choice may lead.

Of course there is a possibility that this first assessment will raise questions or even make you question your GO decision. If this happens and you're feeling uncertain about your GO choice, then it's vital to explore the source of those feelings:

- Are your feelings caused by the people you work with or the environment you work in?
- Are they occurring because you discovered things about your GO choice that surprised you once you got there?

- Did you miss something in your previous IDENTIFY stage that was important to your being able to thrive in the new environment?

In every GO decision, we abdicate a certain amount of control over the outcome. *We take a risk!* After all, we are entering an unknown world. That's why it is critical to do a lot of research at the IDENTIFY stage. It also holds true in the ASSESS stage, should it lead you to move sooner than you may have anticipated. Most people enter GO with a one-to-three-year time horizon in mind, but external forces and events can change that. There's no set timeframe for a cycle to last; it is all about you and whether you are continuing to thrive and grow after you have made a GO choice. So, rather than hold to a hard and fast timeline, it's always better to have a sense of what progress is needed in order to grow as a professional.

Deciding to GO is a risk-reward proposition. It involves knowing what you have to risk versus what you desire in return. Keep in mind that reward is not only about money. It involves overall satisfaction, including your lifestyle and how you want to engage with your family, friends, and business colleagues. It also includes your own sense of accomplishment and the things you need to do in order to satisfy the internal reward systems that make up your brain and your personality.

The ASSESS phase is where you can distinguish real opportunities from fanciful notions. (Over time, it also makes subsequent GO decisions more reliable.) This is where you seek, question, read, watch, and hear people who are doing things you imagine would make you happy, gratified, or rewarded. It is not merely a research process. ASSESS is where you ask yourself, in light of the new information you've acquired, whether the path you're on is still the right one to meet your driving need—and *why* you feel that way. One way or another, your feeling will find expression in ways that are undeniable.

Assessing should be an exhaustive process that includes *an honest self-evaluation*. On the surface, you may think you want to be and do something, but in fact you may not have the physical or psychological makeup for it. To be a firefighter, for example, while you may be able to acquire the necessary physical attributes through exercise and strength training, the role requires more. Good firefighters must have a powerful internal drive to defeat life-threatening and property-threatening fires of all kinds. Without that internal drive, most people should not choose to serve in such a demanding and dangerous occupation. Other fields have different demands, but they all require a mental buy-in, a sense of service, in addition to the list of official job requirements. Discovering that sense of service, no matter the level of risk or reward, is a key component of the ASSESS stage.

The IDENTIFY phase is the natural but often unexpected outgrowth of assessing. As you attend events on subjects that interest you, dig into trade associations and networking groups, read business books and biographies of fellow seekers, you will find something that suddenly makes your path clear. You might refer to it as a "goal" for your life, except for the fact that it very often wasn't something you had planned ahead of time.

The IDENTIFY stage, where you begin to recognize the singular NEXT stage of your growth cycle, is extremely personal. The key is to use the research from the ASSESS stage to fully evaluate *where you stand now and where you want to go with your career and your life*. For many of us, our career is synonymous with our life. At a minimum, it is our livelihood. It's a great luxury to be able to choose a livelihood that also fits your idea of how you want to live, so a real IDENTIFY moment has to be more than idle fantasy. Knowing that you'll be contributing more than half of your waking hours to such a livelihood, you need to know that it does more than just provide for basic needs.

Think of this phase not as a ladder but as a road map you picked up while driving through a new part of the country. The map may show you a compelling spot to visit, but there will be different ways to get there. There are direct and scenic routes, but the goal is clear. Along the way, you may find new routes, new leapfrog moments, or the seeds of future adventures, but you will also be better prepared to meet them when they come.

The NEXT phase may seem like a letdown after the excitement of finding the "next big thing," but it's just as important. For some, it may be a subtle, incremental change. For others, it may be an overwhelming, challenging step up in the world. It may also be a complete departure from anything you've done previously. All these possibilities involve finding and seizing an opportunity, and require different levels of study and preparation.

Subtle, incremental, and yet important changes in your career may escape the notice of those around you, even when they're obvious to you. This can involve gradual shifts in social behavior, practices you alter deliberately as you begin to change things around. You don't need to announce to the world that you're changing these things; you just start doing them.

Incremental change, applied methodically and at a reasonable cadence, can pay dividends over a relatively short time. It's certainly more satisfying than the grind of merely toiling at your job and waiting to be recognized. It is a process of continuous improvement, finding places to exercise those skills uncovered in your ASSESS and IDENTIFY phases. An incremental NEXT phase may be as simple as volunteering for more responsibility in your current position before asking for a promotion. This can happen whenever a position above you becomes vacant, and you present your willingness to do more as a savings of time and money—the classic leverage move in middle management.

Of course, the NEXT phase may well involve a highly visible exit from your current position before entering the new one. In those cases, when you know your new destination, it's vital to leave your soon-to-be-former home in good shape for the next occupant. This is not just a legal or ethical requirement in employment situations; it's also pure common sense. Your journey does not take place in isolation, and everything you say or do during a transition will always come back to either bite or bless you during the next round. This means that the final phase can take time and probably try your patience, especially when it involves an exciting leapfrog moment. But it's worth the effort. Leaving the campsite better than you found it, to use a saying from the Boy Scouts, is good for everyone, as your NEXT becomes the GO for a brand-new adventure.

Making the Leap

Finally, as I recounted in Chapter 2, there are usually many opportunities to make unexpected or unanticipated moves within a growth cycle—or from one cycle to another. These events, which I called leapfrog moments, are not contrary to the idea of growth cycles. Rather, they are the "fuel" for growth itself. While they may seem random or arbitrary, in reality they are integral to GAIN. So long as they are real, not just imaginary flights of fantasy, think of leapfrogging as intuitive shortcuts to GO, ASSESS, IDENTIFY, and NEXT.

The easiest way for me to explain leapfrog moves is to look at certain key events in my own career. In hindsight, I am certain these were leapfrog moves, even though at the time I didn't fully realize what I was doing. At a very young age, I pursued something that I thought would yield a profit, through a combination of effort, creativity, and a little bit of money or access. I promoted local bands, made recordings, and got them distributed around town for play on small radio stations. After a year or two of trying this without much success, my leapfrog move was to enter the system by getting a job in broadcasting, where I began to pursue my aspirations incrementally.

My first paying, full-time job was a low-level promotion position at a TV station. I used this exposure, along with my brief experience as a DJ, to make more out of the basic job, adding an element of creativity to produce content that actually got on the air and made an impact—at least on my boss, who took credit for spiking up the promotion department. From there, I gained more freedom to move around and meet people, which led to my first job in sales—my first real leapfrog move.

Being in sales exposed me to the station's top management. It also increased my income, but with the risk that comes with working on commission. Because I was successful, and because management liked me, word got around. I received a series of incremental promotions and account assignments that broadened my circle of contacts. I was recruited for a bigger sales position and a move to a much larger broadcast market. This mattered not only because the job came with a base salary and performance bonuses, but also because it exposed me to other types of media business people—something that would spark future growth cycles.

My exposure to a broader business environment, and to the movements of people from one business situation to another, opened up my view of the world. I began to study the *business* of broadcasting, and realized I needed to learn business and finance. I still had a desire to be something more. That "something more," I realized, was the step from salesman to businessman, which is when I made the biggest leap.

I knew how to sell, but I also I had an inkling that what I wanted to sell was not ads but *business ideas and concepts*. So, I set out to learn everything I could about starting and financing businesses. Once I made this leap and established the mindset of a businessman, the rest became a blur. When I sold my first financing deal, it leveraged me into becoming a business partner, and then a business owner. From there, I was working at an entirely different level.

Later in my career, using these same principles, I leapfrogged from a small private firm into a c-suite position at a large publicly held media company. Then I became executive chairman of a media company owned by one of the largest buyout funds in the world. Each one of these moves was very nontraditional in nature. They came out of my own ASSESS-and-IDENTIFY process, in which I saw opportunities that benefitted my new partners in ways that were not apparent to them at the time.

Exercise for the Reader

As a final exercise, I'm asking you to describe the growth cycle you may be on at this very moment. Even if all the details are not perfectly clear, try to imagine (and write down as much as you can) the things that stand out as your current road map.

1. How would you describe your current situation? How well does it meet your needs—from the basic, physiological needs to the higher, more aspirational needs that all humans have?
2. Is there some move or action that you can take, subtle or otherwise, that would change your current situation AND would resonate positively with you personally?
3. What would you need to know (about yourself and about the situation) to determine that the move or action was the right one?
4. Can you imagine identifying an aspect of that move or action that not only stands out but also serves as a milestone for something greater?
5. If you could identify such a milestone, how do you think you could prepare yourself to actually take that path?

No matter what business you're in, or what position you occupy at the moment, there is always something ahead of or above you that you feel, consciously or not, is worth discovering and achieving. That's simply part of the human condition. But to get there, you cannot remain satisfied with the grind and wait for things to come to you. It's critical to recognize that you're in a growth cycle right now, even if the details or the sequence of events are not perfectly clear. You may also be having unexpected "mindset shifts" that tell you what's really going on. But above all, recognize that each of these events requires something of *you*.

It's not enough just to read about growth cycles and agree with these principles—as I hope you will. It's also not sufficient to daydream, or merely *talk* about GAIN, or procrastinate because you think it's too late. (Spoiler alert: it is never too late.) In order to make the principles of GO, ASSESS, IDENTIFY, and NEXT an integral part of your own growth, you need to actually *do* something, right now, to make the application of growth cycles a lifelong habit.

Acknowledgments

I want to thank everyone I worked with and especially those who gave me the opportunity to prove myself and address the challenges that created growth and success. I also want to thank the many people who worked alongside me or on my teams because I learned how to lead by observing what created the most successful teams and enterprises. I want to thank all of you who influenced, aided, or simply gave me ideas that led to success. There are many of you and I hope in some way you gained from our time together as I surely did.

I also want to thank all the people who resisted or opposed my ideas—the ones who undermined my plans overtly and subvertly, those who stabbed me in the back and in the face, and those who competed with me or just plain didn't like me, because without you I never would have gained the survival tools or mentality to succeed in business at the highest levels.

As my wife always said to me, don't use energy hating on people who wronged you, bless them and turn that energy into fuel and focus on people who lift you up.

I leave you with this. Stefan Pruett closed over a thousand shows around the world with the following exhortation: "Onward and upward! Greatness abounds!"

Music Credits

Once In A Lifetime
Words and Music by Brian Eno, David Byrne, Christopher Frantz, Jerry Harrison and Tina Weymouth
Copyright © 1980 by EG Music Ltd., WC Music Corp. and Index Music, Inc.
All Rights for EG Music Ltd. in the United States and Canada Administered by Universal Music - MGB Songs
All Rights for Index Music, Inc. Administered by WC Music Corp.
International Copyright Secured All Rights Reserved
Reprinted by Permission of Hal Leonard LLC

ONCE IN A LIFETIME
Words and Music by DAVID BYRNE, CHRIS FRANTZ, JERRY HARRISON, TINA WEYMOUTH and BRIAN ENO
© 1980 WC MUSIC CORP., INDEX MUSIC, INC. and E.G. MUSIC LTD.
All Rights on Behalf of itself and INDEX MUSIC, INC. Administered by WC MUSIC CORP.
All Rights Reserved
Used by Permission of ALFRED MUSIC

If I Ever Was A Child
Words and Music by Jeffrey Tweedy
Copyright © 2016 Words Ampersand Music
All Rights Administered by BMG Rights Management (US) LLC
All Rights Reserved Used by Permission
Reprinted by Permission of Hal Leonard LLC 2

About the Author

Steven J. Pruett is executive chairman of Cox Media Group. Before joining CMG, Pruett served as executive vice president and chief TV development officer of Sinclair Broadcast Group, where he had also served as vice president and co-chief operating officer. Pruett was responsible for creating the company's Chesapeake Division through acquisitions, as well as overseeing all TV stations in that group.

Before joining Sinclair, Pruett was chief financial officer for Communications Corporation of America and later became its president and CEO. Prior to that, he was a special strategic advisor to DirecTV and Thomson Consumer Electronics.

Over a long, successful career, Pruett has helped found several broadcast groups as an initial investor, financier, managing partner, or board member. These include Spanish Radio Group, Excel Communications, ACME Television, USBG, and UPI Media, where he served as president. He also served as treasurer of the FOX Affiliate Board of Governors and was elected chairman.

Pruett studied radio and television at Southern Illinois University in Edwardsville. He earned a master's in management from the Kellogg School of Management at Northwestern University. He lives in Atlanta and Arizona with his wife, Paula.